Preserved open space

or costly urban sprawl?

Local governments in rapidly developing

urban regions must face this

critically important

CHALLENGE OF THE LAND

by Charles E. Little

An Open Space Action Institute Report
for municipal officials and civic leaders

The Open Space Action Institute was formed in 1963 as the Open Space Action Committee. The change of name took place in 1968. The purpose of the Institute—a non-profit, non-governmental corporation—is to encourage the preservation of open space in and around urban areas by means of field programs, publications and technical services. Up to now its most notable field activity has been the "Stewardship Program" dealing with landowners in the tri-state New York Metropolitan Region. Currently a new "Municipal Program" is underway. Projects and minor programs have been undertaken elsewhere in the U.S. on a limited basis. In the years ahead, OSAI anticipates greater involvement in all major metropolitan centers of the country.

Publications include, beside *Challenge of the Land, Stewardship: the Land, the Landowner, the Metropolis, Open Space Preservation Methods* (an edited conference proceedings report) plus a series of "Open Space Action Reports" to be inaugurated in 1968 and, from time to time, the issuance of staff monographs concerned with various aspects of land preservation. All these are available from the Institute's headquarters office. Field programs and publications are undertaken by a professional staff made possible through Foundation grants and private contributions, which are tax deductible.

OPEN SPACE ACTION INSTITUTE

145 EAST 52 STREET, NEW YORK, N. Y. 10022

(212) 421-0732

Foreword

It was only a few years ago—in 1964—that Charles E. Little faced his first big challenge. The Open Space Action Committee was less than a year old, and it was up to Little (then, as now, its chief executive officer) to spank some life into the infant. He did that, sitting at a desk in the basement of his home near Peekskill, N. Y., with one file drawer and a sheaf of maps hung on a concrete-block wall. When the telephone rang for Little upstairs, as it often did, he listened for the signal from his wife Katie: two stomps on the kitchen floor above. And that's really how this book began.

The stomping is over. Little's desk, now in a Manhattan office building, sits seven stories high over East 52nd Street. The staff has grown to a point where it occupies half a floor of this building. The organization is no longer the "committee." It's the Open Space Action Institute.

Action is what the Institute—and this book—is all about. Since 1963, our field representatives have initiated projects involving the preservation of some $10 million worth of privately-owned open space to public, or quasi-public, uses—parks, sanctuaries, stream valley easements, natural areas. In one recent OSAI project, a 134-acre estate was turned into an ecology study center, so that today's graduate may become tomorrow's active conservationist.

Sometimes it seems that conservation today—the *new* conservation—isn't active enough. There is plenty of rhetoric, and breast-thumping and bell-ringing. But where does it all lead? As Little himself notes on one of the pages that follow, ". . . no policy document has ever saved an acre of land." Action has. And action clearly is needed. Though Charles Little and his staff have been involved in preserving open space amounting to 2,000 acres in the New York metropolitan region each year, urban sprawl in this same region now claims forever the same amount of open space *each week*.

There is a word for preservation action that has been popularized by the Institute: Stewardship. That was Little's second challenge, convincing the private owners of the region's remaining woods, fields, streams, lakes and marshes that they, in fact, are stewards of the land, and that their decisions about the land would irrevocably shape the region's future environment. So Charles Little sat down at his desk (in a file room on 42nd Street, this time) and wrote a book called *Stewardship: the Land, the Landowner, the Metropolis.* In it, he explained how a landowner, philanthropically inclined, might donate open space to a recreation agency or conservation organization, how another might develop his property without sacrificing its natural values, and how, through open space easements, an owner might resist the allure of development, continue to live on his land and, at the same time, stabilize his rising property taxes. Published by the Institute in December 1965, *Stewardship* was hailed by The New York Times as a major contribution to the literature of practical conservation. And the executive director of The Nature Conservancy said of it: "It is an excellent publication and ought to have as great an impact as anything yet published." But the book was more than that, or rather, became more than that as nearly 10,000 copies were placed in the hands of potential "stewards" in the New York region. For those who have asked, "With what results?," Charles Little can point with pride to most of those thousands of acres that shall remain forever green, largely because of that book.

And now, with this, his second book, and the beginning of the Institute's Municipal Program, the author walks the other side of the street where (as he has warned) the obstacles are higher, the pitfalls deeper than any encountered in the Stewardship Program. Municipalities are more complex than individuals, if only because each one is a conglomerate of many individuals, some who fully understand the values of open space, but mostly those who do not. The purpose of this book is not simply to enlighten those who do not, but to teach those who do appreciate open space values how to turn that appreciation into positive open space acquisitions.

In a stricter sense, this book is for county and municipal officials—planners, park commissioners, conservation advisors, administrators and educators, and all the members of all those diverse boards and agencies functioning in every community. It is also for those civic leaders who prod and cajole their elected officials, for better or for worse, into decisions affecting the use of open spaces. Fortunately, there has been a growing concern among municipal officials for open space preservation in recent years. And in a few lucky communities, decision-makers are beginning to eschew the old philosophy that a single-family house on every lot is tax money in the treasury.

With the cost of municipal services increasing, it just doesn't work that way any more. What does work? Open space.

I recommend this book to everyone in or out of government. It is a short book, and that's good. With so much to do, with so little urban and suburban open space left to preserve, there's not much time for reading. So read quickly then, and take a fresh look at your own community. You might be surprised by the opportunities you see there.

JAMES B. ROSS
President
Open Space Action Institute

Table of Contents

Preface

There was a time—and not so long ago at that—when the "challenge of the land" involved beating back the wilderness, homesteading, forging westward across a roadless continent, establishing thriving settlements where only Indian villages had stood before.

To this enterprise, the early settlers and pioneers brought a zeal tinged with moral and religious fervor. The establishment of civilization was, on its face, Good. The primeval forest, the virgin prairie sod, resisting the axe and single ploughshare, seemed, because they stood in opposition to man, Bad.

But yard by yard, acre by acre, mile by mile, the continent gave way. This early challenge of the land was met. Man with his strength and will prevailed over nature and much of the continental United States capitulated to civilization completely. But man turned out to be a not very noble victor. When Nature was on her back, he kept stomping and stomping until in some places there was nothing left. "I can lime it, crossplough it, manure it and treat it with every art known to science," President Franklin Delano Roosevelt said of his place in Hyde Park, New York, according to historian Arthur Schlesinger, Jr., "but the land has just plain run out—and now I am putting it into trees in the hope that my great grandchildren will be able to try raising corn again."

In the twentieth century, man has been discovering, too slowly, that an utterly vanquished natural environment is not what he wanted at all; and that in killing it, he has killed a part of himself. Thus, a new challenge of the land has emerged. So far this challenge has been met with some success in two settings: many remaining wilderness areas are protected by our great national park system, and in our agricultural areas new conservation techniques have brought some of the "run out" land back into productivity. But there is a third setting where the challenge has not been met—in our burgeoning metropolitan areas.

There is a part of every city where it is too late, where the natural environment is buried under so many yards of concrete and asphalt that except for the few city parks, only wholesale urban reconstruction would suffice. But beyond the cores of cities are vast areas where the element of choice is still very much alive, where the city is still being built.

In the New York metropolitan region, with which this book will mainly deal, more than half the population lives outside the city limits of New York itself. Here there are 550 separate municipal governments. Their total land area in three states is 6,600 square miles compared to New York City's 300 square miles. As a result, there is a multiplicity of small decisions concerning land-use which together make up the mammoth decision of whether urban man can live in harmony with nature or will continue, in the building of cities, to stomp it to death.

Every time a planning board meets, or a conservation commission, or a borough council, or a board of selectmen, choices are being made either by design or default. The making of these choices is the contemporary "challenge of the land." The option is for urban sprawl and all its concommitant evils—ugliness, sub-standard living conditions, inefficiency, high tax rates; or for preserved open space. That is, for community development where nature remains as an integral part.

There is a saying among planners, conservationists and others who sincerely hope the right path will be taken: "Everybody is for open space, *but* . . ." Open space is easy to be for, but actual preservation is hard to put into practice. It is not necessary to be cynical. Open space is being preserved in imaginative new ways. That is what this report is all about.

The thesis presented here is that the challenge of the land is fundamentally a municipal concern and, further, that proven techniques of open space preservation constitute the single most viable tool for meeting the challenge.

The Open Space Action Institute wishes to thank all those who have been so helpful in the preparation of this report. They need not be mentioned here, for they are cited in the text. Special acknowledgement is owed to Linda A. Murray and Ned C. Smith of the Open Space Action Institute staff. They were more than helpful to the author in the process of research and writing.

C. E. L.

Chapter I.

Coming to Grips

Jack Keogh is a municipal employee with the title of "Administrative Assistant to Boards and Commissions." He works for the Town of Ramapo in suburban Rockland County. Keogh is young, energetic and talks to his visitor rapid-fire about his town, its troubles and what is being done about them. His story can serve as a good introduction to the ways a municipality can respond to crisis.

It all started here in Ramapo in 1956, Keogh says. *That's when the Tappan Zee Bridge and the New York Thruway really pulled the cork for this county and our town in particular. We didn't know what to do. People just came flooding in. The growth from 1950 to 1960 was up 130% and most of that in the latter part of the decade. Over the next twenty years population will double.*

What Happened in Ramapo

When John MacAlevey ran for Supervisor in 1965, his platform was "controlled growth." He really hit the electorate on the head with that one. We've been having terrific problems because of too rapid development. Drainage problems, lots of crummy developments, highway mess, taxes. Taxes have reallly gone through the roof. In one school district of the town they went up 25% last year. That's what subdivision does to you. The typical home owner in that district has to pay something like $1,000 a year in taxes these days.

After John got in office, the first thing we did was tighten up on the building permits, really give them a good going over to see that everything was on the up and up, particularly with reference to drainage. We decided we had to have a full-time engineer, something we've never had.

We established a drainage commission* which administered a set of very specific regulations: no filling of streams, diverting, that kind of thing. Also existing conditions that might lead to flooding had to be corrected.

* See Appendix A for Legislation

1

All this time we were working on a new master plan. We had zoning, of course, but the new master plan was to call for up-zoning certain areas of the town. We could see that just as soon as this was generally known, builders would be hustling to get in under the wire. So in June of 1966 we passed an "Interim Development Law"* which was in essence a building freeze, protecting the integrity of the master plan until we could have all the hearings necessary and get its zoning provisions passed into law.

There were a lot of threats and the opposition ran ads accusing us of dictatorship, but the thing stuck. The law was upheld in the New York Supreme Court and is now in the Appellate Division. We did have a way out, of course, by providing that builders could apply for relief to the Town Board. Although the law was not completely arbitrary, the Board didn't release many large tracts. The new zoning went into effect in December, 1966 and the Interim Development Law was automatically out of business. By and large the plan up-zoned vacant land by one step: R-15 to R-25, R-25 to R-35, that sort of thing.

Also in 1966 we revised our average density law.† Before, the law allowed the builder a 20-30% reduction in lot size if the left-over land were set aside for municipal purposes. We didn't think it provided enough flexibility from a design or an open space standpoint; so we did away with arbitrary standards except that the minimum lot size would have to be 15,000 square feet. But this could apply in an R-80 zone as well as an R-25. However, in an R-15 zone we'll permit 12,000 square feet.

But the most important thing about the new average density law is that it now permits the planning board to require density averaging in order to preserve certain areas —this is particularly important along water courses.

The latest thing we're doing is DEACOM—the "Development Easement Acquisition Commission."‡ This is based

* Appendix B
† Appendix C
‡ Appendix D

2

on New York's General Municipal Law, Section 247*
which provides that a town can accept less than fee rights
in open land and in return provide property tax relief.
With this Commission, the town can make an agreement
with a large landowner that if he won't develop his prop-
erty, then his property tax can reflect a reduced valuation
on the land. We had a general re-assessment in 1963, so
property owners are beginning to feel the pinch. We're
afraid they will sell out too fast and this new law can help
us control the rate of development at least, if not preserve
some open space in perpetuity.

We got a fair amount of flak in the hearings. One person
made a big speech about how the idea was "Marxism," but
he was practically laughed out of the hall. Some people
were afraid that politics would get into the Commission's
deliberations, so we made sure that the group would be a
fair cross-section of the community.

All in all, we've been trying very hard to get at this
problem of too-rapid growth. A town like Ramapo just
can't keep up with the service demands, number one;
and number two it just won't be a fit place to live in unless
we can combat this urban sprawl. We've been sticking our
necks out pretty regularly for the last few years, but
that's what you have to do if you expect to have anything
left. A lot of people worry that what we might accomplish
will just be temporary, that somebody else will come along
and sell off the open space and the stream valleys and so
forth. I don't. I think you've got to believe that there will
be good guys in the future in municipal government.

What Keogh provides here is an inventive catalogue of
actions that a municipal government can take to help control rampant urbanization. It is a good example of the kind
of processes a creative government can initiate.

If Ramapo is unusual in its response, it is perfectly
ordinary in its problem. What has been happening in
Ramapo has been happening all over the New York Metropolitan Region and other urban areas throughout the

* Appendix E

country. Everywhere, municipal officials and civic leaders have had to come to grips with urbanization which like time and tide waits for no man. The forms of coming to grips might very well differ markedly from Ramapo. But the stimulus is the same, and the degree of involvement of municipal government can certainly be no less.

Population Growth The phenomenon of post-war urbanization has been called "spread city" by the Regional Plan Association, which measured it for the New York region in 1962 and made some startling projections. Suffolk County, for example, will double in population by 1985. But more surprising is that it will be second in population only to Brooklyn of all the New York region counties. It will exceed Queens, the Bronx and teeming Manhattan itself. The urbanization of such outlying areas as Suffolk and Rockland County (which incidentally projects a 110% increase between now and 1985) means the city will measure one hundred miles across and its edges will be indistinguishable from the next city down, or up, the line. Even today there are commuters in Princeton, New Jersey who depart in different directions each morning—one set to Philadelphia, another to New York. Also it is becoming more and more difficult to locate the line which marks the edge of the suburb or exurb and the pure unadulterated countryside. In 1962, the Regional Plan Association was satisfied to define the region as twenty-two counties. In its most recent study, *The Region's Growth*, published in 1967 as a part of the "Second Regional Plan," the region grew suddenly from 22 counties to 31, which now has a population of 19 million and by the year 2000 will have a population of 30 million.

But population statistics are, by themselves, meaningless. What really counts is how they interact with the land supply. This interaction is controlled by economic and sociological forces all of which are twisted up with the "American Dream," the flickering images of grass, trees and "a good place for the kids to grow up."

4 It is a dream which is presently being shattered by the

cataclysmic forces of urbanization. The metropolitan countryside is beginning to emerge more and more as a nightmare. Instead of the charming little house in the country there is the monotony of uninspired development. Instead of pleasant country roads, the thoroughfares have become bizarre strips of gas station after gas station, shopping center after shopping center. Brooks have become so culverted that no one remembers them, ponds are polluted and sometimes just dry up. The landscape is festooned by high tension wires and slashed by new highways that chew up an incredible fifty acres of land per mile.

To add insult to injury, as paradise diminishes it costs more and more to live there. A new 100-house subdivision can require the construction of a new elementary school, and these days the costs for such structures are in the million dollar category. In the New York Region, public educational facilities will cost over $10 billion in the period 1960-1985. Moreover, every year increased operating costs have to be met—mostly teachers' salaries which now start at $6,000. Taxes must rise, too, for increased municipal service costs—police, fire protection, sewers, road maintenance. In one Westchester town the price tag for refurbishing a handful of local roads was put at $3 million. This did not include widening or new rights of way of any kind. In one Monmouth County town a new sewer system is budgeted at $18 million.

Economic Penalty of Growth

Property taxes are the principal source of revenue for educational and municipal services. When these taxes increase, land is forced into development for it loses its appeal as investment and becomes an impractical luxury even for the rich. High property taxes can have a depressing effect in respect to the marketability of land in large chunks. The problem feeds on itself, its capacity for landscape obliteration ever increasing.

And because of the specialized nature of the metropolitan countryside, the worst is yet to come. The dominant pattern of suburban development has centered on the single family house. This is the financial root of the problem since

5

such domiciles are attractive to families with children and since children are so expensive to educate. Actually, in the 60's the urban fringe has been having it pretty easy—although it would be hard to convince most municipal officials and civic leaders of that fact. According to the Regional Plan Association it is the age group 30-34 who are the most avid buyers of single family housing. And this age group has been declining as a component part of the total population in the decade of the sixties. Indeed, in 1970 it will be 7% lower than in 1960. But after 1970, watch out! At that moment it will start to be an increasingly larger part of the whole—and the "whole" will be increasing rapidly too. Therefore the suburbs are in for a double whack: population growth generally and specifically from the post-war babies now reaching that period when they want and need the land and services—particularly educational—that only the metropolitan countryside can supply.

The big question that arises is, can the suburbs survive this onslaught and still be suburbs? Will there still be grass, trees, a "good place for the kids to grow up?" Or is the American Dream a fake?

If the status quo cannot be maintained—and it can't—then what is there to do except lie back and get paved over? If the tax base just refuses to be balanced no matter how much hopeful rezoning you do for "clean industry" or "lab-office," what is there except to be grateful for the strings of gas stations, the ersatz ice-cream stands and the other plastic whatnots of commerce-in-suburbia which unlike houses don't send 2.5 children to school? Is the metropolitan countryside's only use to be chopped first—then to be minced—and finally to be powdered like an onion?

The Function of Suburbia   When municipalities are engaged with the problems of the moment, it is easy to forget what the suburban function is in the metropolitan scheme of things, which is (again) grass, trees and a good place for the kids to grow up. For some suburbs it is too late, no doubt. They have become basically urban—their only point of difference being that they are built a little bit closer to the ground than the central city. The *critical* difference between the central city and the countryside which surrounds it is, of course, the presence of a more or less natural environment where hills are still hills, and woods remain unscathed by bulldozers.

There's been a high, hot wind blowing up from the Potomac and from various state capitals about "natural beauty." And indeed there have been some interesting programs set up, however underfinanced. Nothing is served by disparaging the propaganda apparatus of the "Great Society." But municipal leaders should be disabused of any notion that the preservation of the natural environment in the metropolitan countryside will be achieved, finally, by a bureaucrat dashing in at the last moment on a white horse to pluck the urban fat from the suburban fire by showering town hall with thousand dollar bills.

And that brings it down to the hard nut of the matter. Whose responsibility is the environment? And, does the quality of the environment have some kind of connection with the fiscal health of the community?

The answers to these questions are as follows: (1) Municipal government; (2) Yes.

The land, of course, is the key as Ramapo and other communities are finding out. Municipal government can't make a silk purse out of a sow's ear, but where at least some land is uncommitted to urban uses (and in most "ring" counties this is the greatest part) local governments have greater power over land use decisions than anyone else. They control the land because they can zone it, tax it, buy it, sell it. And if they do a good job they can affect the physical environment in a way that is profoundly significant to all the people who live in their community, work in their community, or even pass through their community.

But this is perhaps a self-evident truth. The bind comes in money, and here, too, the land is the key. Some land uses are profitable. Some can be a dead loss. Some land uses increase the total value of the community. Some land uses depreciate the value of the community.

Land is the Key

7

Now no municipal government can operate like a French King and decree that the town shall be beautiful and that its treasury shall grow without civil strife. Limiting the range of choices are restrictions relating to such details as the constitutional rights of landowners, fair tax practices, political realities, and traditional economic and social forces.

What's needed is some kind of environmental *focus:* an action capability which provides a direction for the municipality to follow in threading its way through the complex environmental and fiscal problems of community growth.

Open Space: The Environmental Focus

That focus *has* to be open space, for open space is the palpable difference between countryside and core. The open space in question here is not limited to the little green blobs found on master plans—the "701 specials" in the files of most municipal offices. *What open space means is the present total of the natural environment in a given municipality.*

And this is the point of leverage a municipality has. The minute a municipal official sees the vacant, uncommitted land in his community not as something to be filled up with the what-nots of urbanization, but as a natural resource to be husbanded, parcelled out grudgingly, cleverly used to produce economic benefits, and yes, *conserved*, he has made a remarkable discovery. He has found the focus for decision-making and the instrument by which he can at once produce a more desirable physical environment *and* a greater degree of fiscal health, for one follows the other invariably.

Most municipalities, like Ramapo, are beginning to make this discovery, and in making it, are coming to grips with the problems of growth.

Chapter II.

The Case for Open Space Preservation

While almost any municipal official will agree to the general principle that open space should be preserved rather than needlessly destroyed, the translation of sentiment into official action is another matter. Therefore, it is the *rationale* of open space that must concern the municipal official, and whatever philosophical views he may have are perhaps not as relevant as they might be in a better world. The people have to be *sold*.

Lists of open space benefits have become popular in recent years among planners and preservationists alike and the official must approach open space, over all, in terms of some kind of basic function. When all is said and done, there are basically three.

The first is for the establishment of recreational opportunity.

The Three Functions of Open Space

The second is for the establishment of attractive community design, a visually pleasant landscape, and the environmental amenity this supplies.

The third is for the maintenance of natural processes, or, in a word, conservation.

Each of these three basic approaches to open space have inherent physical, social and economic benefits, and though in many cases all three functions can be served by one piece of land (or one *system* of open space), they can be discussed separately.

The municipal role in providing land for outdoor recreation is relatively new. The town park as the be all and end all of municipal open space served well for quite a long time. While there was gradual change as the country industrialized, a middle class emerged, and working hours decreased somewhat, nothing much had to be done about it until America's "new society" began in 1946 at the close of World War II.

Outdoor Recreation

More children were produced than at any other time in

9

history. Labor had discovered during the war how to put management over a barrel and hours were shortened and paychecks fattened. Management had learned how to really produce the goods in a more efficient way than ever before. Everybody wanted a house in the country, and the VA (and FHA) decreed that it could be so. Everybody wanted an education and the Veterans Administration decreed that it could be so, also. So everyone got more money, more children and more time off. On this base post-war America has been built and is expanding in a geometric progression. The three components of its growth more people, more money, more leisure time.

It is not too much to say that this caught most municipalities flat-footed. It continues to catch them flat-footed. Because no matter how splendidly the Federal Government performs in creating National Parks, or State Government performs in creating State Parks—most of these facilities are by their nature resource-oriented.* No matter how grand the Grand Canyon, it can't mean much to the average surburbanite except once or twice in his life time. What is he going to do with his 2,920 free hours of time year in and year out? Thus, today, recreationists argue for outdoor opportunities where the people are, or as close to them as can possibly be arranged, so that the opportunity can be at least weekly, if not daily.

As a result, municipalities are having to get into the act. Most counties and most towns are beginning to provide for the close-to-home, day-use kind of recreation, which can be realized only through the preservation of open space for that purpose.

Free recreation is practically a thing of the past. The old swimming hole is now posted against trespassers if not filled in by a development and the benches at the town park are just not going to do for the variety of recreational experiences that the increasing numbers of moneyed, leisured residents demand.

To put the calipers on this demand and to give a self-

* Recently, however, New York State has set up a
10   Commission for State Parks in New York City.

evident crisis official status, President Eisenhower appointed the Outdoor Recreation Resources Review Commission, (ORRRC) established by act of Congress in 1958. For four years this commission inventoried existing outdoor recreation areas, projected future demand, learned what people really wanted to do with all their leisure time. The final report came out to a summary plus 27 books.

The report put numbers on what most municipal officials already knew was happening. The population will double before the century is out, and recreational demand will triple. This is because the per capita disposable income will go up from $2,900 to $4,100, while the work week will diminish from 36 hours to 32. Not only that, paid vacations will increase from 2.8 weeks to 3.9 weeks.

The Statistics of Recreational Demand

The reports also documented another fact that most officials instinctively know: there has to be a range of activities provided. The tennis courts at the school grounds do provide open space and a recreational outlet, but what about swimming, which will be the most important pursuit by the end of the century? Moreover, there seems to be a drift away from what one observer called "organized sweating," group activities and team sports. The solitary pursuits and family oriented activities are just as important, such as fishing, walking in the woods, bicycling, picknicking, camping, boating.

Two further points that the report makes can provide insight to municipalities. The first is that water is a prime focal point for outdoor recreation. "Wherever they live," writes Frank Gregg in a digest of the report, "most people seeking the outdoors look for water—to swim and fish in, to boat on, to walk, picnic and camp by, and just to look at. The demand for water-based recreation is increasing more rapidly than the demand for outdoor recreation in general.

The other point is a kind of caveat, found in the Summary Report itself. "Parks and other recreation areas are only part of the answer. The most important recreation of all is the kind people find in everyday life. Do the children have to be driven to school—or can they walk or cycle to

11

it safely over wooded paths? Are there streams for an afternoon's fishing—or have they all been buried in concrete culverts? Are the stands of woods all gone—or are a few left for a picnic or a stroll? What this means, in short, is a recreation environment. Thus, our challenge: can we shape future growth so that recreation is an integral part of it?"

A recreation environment, as ORRRC calls it, is a natural environment. And a natural environment serves not only recreation, but equally the need for pleasant, liveable communities.

The Case for Amenity   In fact, the need for community amenity should be considered a function in itself and here too, the natural environment is the key factor. If the arguments for open space based on providing healthful outdoor activity for an increasing number of an increasingly leisured population is the province of the recreationist, the arguments for open space as a design component in a rapidly urbanizing community is the province of the planners and architects.

What worries them, and everybody else too, is the malevolent development now called "slurbs." The cradle of slurban civilization is Los Angeles, California, but its offspring have found congenial soil in the New York region and elsewhere. Slurbia (eating away at the landscape at the rate of 2,000 acres a week in the New York region) is caused by a surprising amalgam of forces. One of these forces is the highly developed profit motive of what may be the last of the rough-and-tumble entrepreneurs in this country, the subdividers/developers, combined with the underdeveloped taste of a swelling market of young buyers more concerned with the equipment in the kitchen than with the larger environment of their new community. To this mix are added well-meant institutions such as the FHA (which has lately mended its ways), and mortagage banks slow to accept any departure from the hackneyed level of development. Another problem: rigid large lot zoning has resulted in a greater amount of bulldozed land for fewer people than any civilization has yet devised.

12

"In suburban areas of one and two story detached buildings," says landscape architect Garrett Eckbo, "we tend to get an equal balance between houses, trees, streets, and ground forms. This produces, especially in the new mass subdivisions, a monotonous pepper-and-salt landscape without variation in scale or character. The monotonous feeling is aggravated by a tendency for streets to become wider, thus increasing the percentage of asphalt in the total landscape." Planners have estimated that this proportion often reaches 30%. That's a lot of asphalt when one subdivision is laid next to another. The image of slurbia that drives the designers mad, and with good reason, is the total municipality consisting of 30% asphalt, 30% lawn and 30% rooftop. The ten per cent is what they get to plan for.

The answer proposed by those of a design persuasion is, of course, to relieve this monotony with chunks, strips, buffers, wedges and ribbons of open space in which the natural environment is a larger component than the 30-30-30-10 ratio would permit. It would be a component that separated neighborhoods, gave structure to individual subdivisions as well as the community as a whole and provided an intimate connection with the natural environment to all the people of the town. "The predominant form of urban open space has been the traditional park," says William L. Slayton, Executive Vice-President of Urban America, Inc. "But there is a vision of cities in which these lands could play a far wider role by providing a continuous green thread of nature interwoven throughout the entire fabric of our urban environment."

Thus the planner presents a rationale for open space that derives from a different point of view than the recreationist, although they both agree with each other more often than not. One perceives open space as mitigating the excesses of urbanization through design, the other through healthful outdoor activities. They are joined by another eager, brighteyed idealist, decked out in high boots and corduroys: the naturalist. He should not be dismissed too quickly as a mere zealot. His arguments have particular 13 cogency for the urbanizing municipality suddenly confronted with channel widening, dredging, riprapping, replanting, ponding and those consequent punishments doled out by Mother Nature when man interferes too clumsily with her seamless web.

Natural Processes The naturalist sees open space as a necessity in order to maintain natural processes in a relatively stable equilibrium. While he believes conservation to be meritorious for its own sake (if not an ethical imperative), he is not averse to pointing out some of the benefits of putting his philosophy into practice.

As urbanization plunges into the countryside all sorts of fascinating things begin to happen. Take the typical case of a rural stream valley. As urbanization proceeds, the summer places become converted to year-round residences, new houses appear here and there, but nothing much is changed. Deer leap about, waves of warblers appear each spring and fall. The red fox is sighted now and again, and along the banks of the stream one may find an otter slide, a muskrat den.

All in all, it is a naturalist's paradise, trillium, mocassin flower, spotted sandpiper and all. Mother Nature has gracefully accommodated minor intrusions of man.

But as the hunter, the angler and the birdwatcher roam about in pleasurable oblivion, a surveyor has just unwittingly declared war on Mother Nature. His new plot plan for a hillside development overlooking the stream valley has just been approved. Soon the bulldozers swing into action. They seem innocuous enough, for it is just one development, but it unleashes a series of events that no one except a naturalist is likely to have foreseen. The land is stripped of topsoil, and new roofs add to positive run-off during the rains. The stripped land cannot absorb the water. It floods into the stream carrying with it tons of silt. Thus because porous topsoil has been removed and positive run-off increased, groundwater levels in that area decline and some folks have to dig deeper wells. Meanwhile, downstream, higher water levels flood basements, and even more important, septic systems fail at time of flood, polluting the water and leading to the danger of hepatitis. A sewer district has to be established. In time the municipality decides that the best thing to do is to dredge the channel to carry the run-off somewhere else. Shortly afterward, a community downstream is hit by a devastating flood, because the normally placid stream has overrun its banks and put a whole housing development underwater. The development was built not in the original flood plain of the stream but in a newly created flood plain. Thus the County decides that the only thing to do is to build a dam and calls the Army Corps of Engineers. Meanwhile upstream, the ground water feeding the wells finally gives out, and a new water supply has to be developed. More dams are planned. But ultimately, that stretch of the stream is all but dried up in the hot months. A water district is established with a complex of pump houses and mains. As urbanization increases it becomes just as easy, after all, to put the stream into a pipe because it isn't much more than a dry ditch anyway much of the year. Mother Nature's retribution finally becomes complete when each spring muddy water bubbles up out of storm drains, and everyone wonders why.

The naturalists argue for a bit less tampering. Not only to preserve the trillium and spotted sandpipers, but also because it is cheaper that way. A ten acre marsh, says naturalist Richard H. Pough, will accommodate 3,000,000 gallons of water in a one foot rise. Take away the marsh and the water has to go somewhere else. The evaporation of an acre of red maples in a moist habitat, says biologist John Bardach, may give off water equivalent to 28 inches of rain in a year. Much better, he says, to leave certain land alone: "Proper land use and flood control are intimately related. In many instances, especially wooded slopes, the best use that can be made of land is to leave it under its natural cover."

By best use, Bardach refers both to the best use for the naturalist as well as the best use according to the receiver of taxes. The argument can come down to money, pure and simple.

The naturalist would be the last to say that nature is in such fragile equilibrium that her temple must never be invaded by man. Nature can restore equilibrium after a fashion. Watersheds can, under proper management, often return to a balance that at least approximates that with which they started. Man and nature can coexist. All the same, there is a threshold as the example above suggests, which can set off a chain of events that if nothing else is terribly costly. The price of flood control, pollution abatement, and similar remedies for land and water abuses is uniformly greater than the price of land control in the first place.* Channel widening, artificial impoundments, dams and the whole list of hydrological maneuvers available provide at great cost what Mother Nature usually provides free of charge if left to her own devices.

For the naturalist, equilibrium brings many benefits, both financial and spiritual. And he feels, rightly enough, that if a municipality is not persuaded by the intrinsic ethic of preserving trillium, mocassin flower and the spotted sandpiper for their own sake, then perhaps they will understand that these living things symbolize a healthy physical environment and if driven out leave a curse on the place they have left.

How to Establish Priorities

The talisman of the naturalist is wildlife, of the planner, amenity, and of the recreationist, outdoor activity. But which should the municipality follow? Which open spaces should the municipality preserve (or encourage to be preserved) to meet the needs of natural process, community amenity, outdoor recreation. Which is the most important, what comes first?

The fact is, a municipal official does not have to make this choice. This is because by the mysterious nature of things, the best recreation land is the best conservation

---

* In a study of drainage problems in New Castle County, Delaware, consulting engineers cited land development, improper planning and flood plain encroachment as the culprits. The estimated cost for remedial measures: $11 million.

land is the best amenity land. This hypothesis is arrived at by applying a theory of priority by overlapping functions. When more than one function is served, priority is automatically established. The lowest priority is where only one function is served; the highest where all three functions are served.

Where do these three functions come together? The answer to that question does not necessarily require elaborate inventories by scientists, technicians or sociologists. In most cases empirical reasoning and a careful look at the landscape is enough. The recreationists say that "water is the focal point." Water and related land provide the greatest range of recreational opportunities. They also speak of trails, woodland paths and large unbroken and isolated areas of open space for hiking and camping. The designer is concerned with either separating or unifying communities via predominant natural land forms, such as, yes, water courses, also ridgelines for visual amenity and large tracts of land to serve as buffers or green belts. The ecologist finds wildlife in greatest abundance near, in and associated with (again) water. He is also concerned with the action of water on vegetation and soil; thus steep slopes require natural cover. Finally, the ecologist knows that many large tracts are necessary because an ecosystem—that is, the integrated plant/animal community that makes up a self-sufficient biological interrelationship—cannot exist with any integrity without preserving certain critical areas undisturbed by what he calls "installations," i.e., land uses or activities which tend to disrupt the ecological balance.

Now, as recreationists, planners, ecologists begin to communicate with each other, the practical application of these guidelines is beginning to emerge into some fairly simple precepts. High priority open space should be preserved in systems that are essentially, linear and augmented by big chunks of land wherever they can be found. These linear systems, as well as the big chunks, should be located on or contain surface water, or be part of a ground water system. Also the system should contain distinguished land-

Systems and Chunks

forms such as ridge tops (also linear) and steep slopes.

If these kinds of lands are preserved, by one means or another, all three open space functions can be served, often simultaneously.

Of course, this should not preclude consideration of two-function open space or even one-function open space since there are occasions when such land simply must be set aside. The Sunken Forest—a unique tract of native holly trees which grow dense and big between the dunes of Fire Island—is an example of one-function open space. It is not needed for recreation—public beaches are nearby. Water is not involved. There is no development in the immediate area and thus no valid design function. It is strictly a unique natural area, of importance only to the biologist and a slender minority of the general public curious about such things. But the Sunken Forest *is* unique, a fascinating botanic accident, and its preservation was nothing less than an urgent requirement.

The problem is, all of the foregoing has been qualitative and not generally subject to the kind of simplistic precision demanded by the local critic who might say, for example, "What're you guys going to do, buy up the whole town?"

How Much Open Space? Mindful of this predicament, the conservationist, the recreationist and the planner have all tried to provide so-called "guidelines" to municipal officials even though they are more a gesture to *Realpolitik* than truly responding to the individual complexities of an individual municipality's open space policy.

Nevertheless, the guidelines are helpful, at least in providing specific justification for official action.

To the purist designer, amenity cannot be measured in acres any more than the value of a painting can be measured in square feet of canvas. Ten feet of Zen garden could theoretically serve better than a hundred acre park. The planner, on the other hand, who appropriates the designers' art for use in the arena of public-decision making, has made an effort to quantify needed open space acreage. The

18 Regional Plan Association recommends that overall pre-

served open space in the New York Region be tripled. This amount of land "would result in a permanent reserve comprising 25% of the Region's terrain. Nothing less will provide the Region's prospective 1985 population of 24 million with a liveable physical environment."

In certain instances and with a good measure of discernment, this "gross minimum calculation" might be applied at the municipal level as an extremely rough bench mark. There are, of course, many municipalities which have more than 25% of their land in permanent open space, but still desperately need additional land for park, flood control, buffers or other purposes.

Gross Minimum Calculation

The National Recreation Association (now the National Recreation and Park Association) popularized the now famous "ten acres per thousand" standard a generation ago, and it has served municipal officials well as either a guide or excuse for acquisition decisions ever since. The formula sounds too suspiciously facile to represent anything but an opinion, probably arbitrary, although from an important source. Such a statistic sticks in the mind and with age becomes encrusted with an implication of scientific accuracy.

The acres per thousand technique of communicating open space needs is a good one, however, since it does tend to reflect an increasing population, which a gross minimum percentage does not. The basic problem with the recreational standard is that it deals with only one aspect or use of open space—outdoor recreation. Moreover, it tends to raise nagging questions about who should provide the land. Should the recreational land be regional in nature, under the ownership of Federal, State, or perhaps the County level of government? Or should the standard be the province of local government?

Acres per Thousand

Marion Clawson, an economist with Resources for the Future, Inc., attempted to patch up the deficiencies of the old ten acres per thousand formula by expanding the function of this kind of measurement, and relating it to both a regional as well as local level.

19

Based on studies made of the Baltimore Metropolitan Area, Clawson decided that new standards should be set forth. He recommended that there should be a total of 78 acres of open space of *all* kinds, and for all purposes, for every 1,000 population. Breaking this figure down, Clawson said that more than half of this amount—42 acres per thousand—should be open space land that would serve an entire region such as large State or Federal parks, watersheds and the like. Thirty-six acres per thousand, the remainder, would serve the local population and therefore be the responsibility of local government. He further divided this overall amount into three categories: "public parks and recreation," 14 acres per thousand; "private recreation," 5 acres per thousand (such as a private golf course); and "green space," 17 acres per thousand.

Clawson's formula has the advantage of reflecting greater leisure time now and in the future, as well as the effects of rapid urban expansion into the countryside—two aspects overlooked by the old ten acre standard.

In spite of the greater sophistication of the Clawson formula, its application on the municipal level can still be far from relevant, and in many cases impossible to achieve. Moreover, it still doesn't (on its face at any rate) convey a real sensitivity to an individual municipality, its people or its landscape.

His Scottish practicality offended by all this, Professor Ian McHarg, a landscape architect, planner, teacher (University of Pennsylvania) and an ecology buff, maintains that acreage is no criteria in itself, but a specific consequence of hard-headed criteria that can be applied to any given segment of land, such as a municipality.

Natural Processes as a Determinant

McHarg's approach is basically an ecological one—economically defensible and serving the recreational and design functions of open space as automatic, if residual, benefits of its application.

Natural processes, argues McHarg, should be the basis on which open space decisions are made, as well as general planning decisions reflecting prohibitions against certain types of land uses. If natural processes are maintained in relative equilibrium, all kinds of benefits accrue. The most dynamic and thus major determinant of natural processes is, again, water. If water is kept in equilibrium, then, says McHarg, the chances are that all natural processes are in equilibrium. Thus land-use limitations as well as sites for open space should be selected on the basis of maintaining the integrity of the water regimen. When this is done, the defense of governmental policy need not rest exclusively on arguments such as natural beauty or the provision of X amount of recreational space for Y amount of people— these things are concommitants. The defense can rest upon the work actually performed by water in process: marshes as reservoirs for flood waters, aquifers (sub-surface water bearing strata) as self-perpetuating water storage basins, unbuilt-upon flood plains to avoid economic and physical catastrophe, protected surface water for purification.

By placing restrictions on the use of water-related land, says McHarg, open space can be infused into development as amenity, and recreational sites provided. Therefore, the absolute amount of land that a municipality should preserve as open space can be calculated exactly by studying the water system. McHarg does not suggest that public ownership is required to accomplish this. It can be effected through zoning and the encouragement of certain private uses which by their nature would not interfere with water in process, as well as through acquisition.

According to McHarg's system, high priority open space would include all surface water and riparian lands as far back from the banks or shores as would keep the water body stable. It would include all marshes and wetlands; all flood plains to the 50 year (2% probability of flooding) level. It would include all aquifer recharge areas, where water percolates into the ground. McHarg provides an excellent illustration here. "The aquifer in New Jersey, parallel to the Delaware River has been estimated by the Soil Conservation Service to have a potential capacity of one billion gallons per day. A water value of 12¢ per 1,000 gallons, the price of water in Philadelphia, would be equal to a $40,000,000 value per annum." Capitalized, this makes a fairly valuable as well as irreplaceable chunk of real estate, so long as the recharge areas are not covered over by development.

Steep lands (12° or more) and the ridges which they constitute are also part of the water dynamic and should not be developed since this would contribute to erosion and remove the forest cover which helps water soak into the ground rather than carve gullies and silt up the watercourses below.

McHarg adds woodlands and prime agricultural lands to his list of land where development should be limited. These, although not directly related to the water regimen, help maintain the regional ecology.

Armed with a soils map, a free service of the Soil Conservation Service via its Soil and Water Conservation District Program, a topographical quadrangle from the United States Geological Survey, various hydrological studies and aerial photos (the Tri-State Transportation Commission has aerial maps for most of the New York region), a municipality can work out its own open space resource map. When McHarg did it for the Philadelphia Metropolitan Area he came up with 60% of the land area— a matrix of open space that would permeate the metropolitan region.

One of the most successful city parks in the world is Fairmount Park in the city of Philadelphia itself. McHarg points out that by applying four of his criteria based on water in process, Fairmount turns out to be located exactly where an urban park should be. The criteria are surface water, flood plains, steep slopes and forests and woodlands. "Had these same four criteria been applied to the city at large," says McHarg, "not only would these areas served by Fairmount Park have been blessed, but throughout the entire city a fabric of open space bordering the numerous rivers and creeks would have been retained. Had this been accomplished, the problems of open space and amenity, so insoluable within the city today, would present no problem."

What the officials of Philadelphia did not know in 1856 when the park was established was that in less than a century, the City of Brotherly Love would be part of a great urban mush indistinguishable from contiguous mushes on the north and on the south all along the Atlantic seaboard.

The larger vision of McHarg arrived at by the projection of hindsight into foresight, is not, however academic. Nor does it come too late for those communities where there are still choices to be made. Most important, it suggests a way municipal officials can not only estimate the amount of open space that should be preserved, but also defend acquisition on hard-nosed economic grounds. One of the problems with a democratic society is that taste cannot be arbitrated by government without the ultimate consent of the governed—just like taxes. In spite of the fact that this is most annoying to the would-be taste-makers who appreciate the aesthetics of open space in design, recreation or wildlife preservation, the perceptions of the uninformed public usually operate at the lowest common denominator.

Therefore, the construction of arguments in favor of open space must lean heavily on the statistical, the economic. This is what the recreationist, the conservationist, and the designer have tried to provide. It is true that broad-based public reaction is beginning to set in, caused by wholesale landscape destruction and the sociological problems resulting from unplanned urban development. The trouble is that this reaction generally reaches full howl only when it is too late to do anything about it. The land is all gone, having completely disappeared under what Lewis Mumford calls "low-grade urban tissue."

To stop or at least to check the advance of low grade urban tissue is a vital function of municipal government, and there is no more effective tool than open space for the purpose. The overlapping uses of open space—amenity, recreation, conservation—are discernible public purposes.   23

The quantity and location of land needed to satisfy these functions can be figured out based on the various formulae and methods of the principal proponents of preservation.

What remains, of course, is action. No map, no policy document has ever saved a single acre of land. But official and civic leadership can.

Chapter III.

Direct Acquisition

The American home truth that "you pays your money and you takes your choice" may be applied to any municipal open space program. While preservation techniques that have nothing to do with money will be discussed later on, the element of choice is often lacking. If a municipality wants *that* piece of land for *that* purpose (usually recreational), then the chances are good that it will have to get up the money to buy it. At this stage of the game recreational demand is burgeoning, but so are land prices. Many, if not most, municipalities are understandably timid about getting into anything but minimum level acquisition programs. Officials are inclined to apply kitchen economics not only to municipal services, but also to land purchase, even though they realize that the postponement of purchase may be costly to rectify later on, or worse, impossible. If the source of official timidity is flat-out local poverty, that is one thing. But if the source has to do with political skittishness, that is quite another. The evidence is mounting that taxpayers will not only agree to open space bond issues, but many of them will actively help municipal government campaign for them.

This was a key factor in a recent New Canaan, Connecticut, open space referendum. When veteran First Selectman Charles F. Kelley was first approached by the owner of the last really big chunk of land in town—300 acres—the proposition he heard must have seemed like an offer to get Buckingham Palace free if he would agree to buy the rest of the British Isles. The deal: New Canaan would receive the donation of the fabulous Lloyd-Lapham mansion, plus out-buildings and surrounding grounds, if the town would pick up the tab on 237 acres of remaining land, for $1.5 million. It was estimated that the total package might be worth as much as $2.5 million to a developer. Even so, a million and a half, even in relatively posh New Canaan,

A Big Acquisition: New Canaan

25

could still buy a terrific amount of something else. New schools were needed and a nagging problem having to do with commuter parking still remained to be solved.

But Kelley felt that this opportunity couldn't wait and most of the other town officials agreed with him. So, in early 1967, he appointed a blue ribbon panel (carefully including a minority party leader) to study the proposition and then to sell it to the community. One of the members of this *ad hoc* committee was Conservation Commission Chairman John D. Gunther. Since his retirement as an attorney for Air Reduction Corporation, grey-maned Jack Gunther had seemed more like a silver bullet than a senior citizen in community affairs. For the Lloyd-Lapham deal, he became the committee's supersalesman.

Gunther's first order of business was to produce and distribute the best brochure small money could buy. For this he enlisted the services of Allen M. Whitlock, a fellow committee member who not entirely by accident happened to be a highly placed executive at Ted Bates, Inc., the giant hard-sell advertising agency which has made patent-medicine pitches a genuine folk-art on the home screen.

Bates, which considers a million-dollar client a midget account, fell to with alacrity for a printing budget of $500, none of which would they skim off as commission. The brochure, big-format (8½ x 11), four-page, heavy stock, with pictures, map and text (not too much), was mailed flat to 4,500 residences, pasted in store windows and passed out at club meetings. It was one of Bates' better efforts.

"WILL NEW CANAAN *ALWAYS* HAVE OPEN SPACE?" demanded the headline, and answered it in the best advertising tradition—fact-filled, reason-why copy to support the purchase. "In case you haven't noticed, we're running out of open space. Our population has grown from 8,000 in 1950 to 13,400 in 1960. The State estimates our present population at 20,400. The projected future population is about 28,500, under existing zoning regulations. During the period from 1955 to 1964 alone over 1,600 dwelling units were constructed.

26

"We can understand the reasons for this growth. New Canaan is a beautiful town with open space—woods— meadows. It is a country community; this is why many of us come here to live. But, in spite of all our zoning and planning, there is one fact from which we can't escape. We're running out of open space."

But for Gunther and Kelley, the brochure was only a starting point. Now the *real* hard-sell had to begin: the personal button-holing, the pleas for organizational support, the work with the local newspaper. ("I lived with them," says Gunther). All community organizations were sent a letter which asked them to put news of the referendum in their bulletins or make announcements at their luncheons. And whenever possible, Gunther and Kelley invited themselves to make a talk about the purchase.

"The basic technique we followed," says Gunther, "was to encourage a large vote. We figured the proposition sold itself and if we could inform *everybody* then we had a chance. My theory is the larger the vote, the more intelligent the result." The strategy was rooted in the phenemenon—by no means exclusive to New Canaan—that while a Presidential election could get a 90% turnout, a recent $1.1 million elementary school bond issue had less than 10% (631 ballots) participating in the vote. To Gunther's way of thinking, that left a lot of room for mischief-making if a well-organized minority opposition to the Lloyd-Lapham plan could get up any momentum.

A corollary to this strategy was to avoid being drawn into tangential arguments. Thus, one of the things the Lloyd-Lapham Property Committee did *not* do was to draw up an elaborate plan for the recreational use of the land. "We emphasized that we should get the property first, and then worry about how exactly to use it," Gunther explains. "We whetted their appetites with 'potential' uses, such as putting in a lake, a golf course, developing the buildings for various civic uses. All this served to point up the versatility of the property. But we didn't want to get hung up on the cost of providing these facilities. For this reason, we spent a lot of time hammering home the alternative—development—and how in the end the purchase would have a restraining effect on taxes. Some people just can't understand the costs of growth. We pointed out in our brochure and in our speeches that if this property were to be used by a developer, our taxes would increase far more as a result of additional services needed by the housing development."

Another potential "hang up" was the matter of State and Federal aid. First Selectman Kelley demurred on making application. "They give 40%," he said, "and want 60% of the control." This may not be altogether precise, but the tactic of no-grants-wanted side-stepped what might have turned out to be one of those "tangential arguments" around which the opposition might coalesce, although the argument has been successfully met in many communities where the need for grant assistance is greater. It is undemocratic, but some suburbanites would just as soon have a pig in the parlor as outlanders in their parks, which is hard to avoid under the terms of most State and Federal grants. While grant-making authorities permit differential fees, they won't permit exclusion of non-residents.

Vote day—Wednesday, July 19, 1967—drew near and the tempo stepped up as nervousness on the part of proponents increased. First Selectman Kelley, Gunther and the rest of the committee were determined to keep the opposition from finding out about each other and to get out as large a vote as possible. Gunther assured members of the Kiwanis club, some of whom were concerned about development costs, that each and every development proposal would be subject to a separate hearing for approval. Proponents of the plan worked the commuter trains, urging everyone to vote.

The message took. The opposition remained scattered, and when the ballots were counted, 2,211 had turned out, approving the plan by 2,098 for and only 113 against—better than seventeen to one. Gunther's theory—"the larger the vote, the more intelligent the result"—was vindicated.

Perhaps the most important point about the New Canaan experience is that lately it seems so unremarkable. Municipalities have been passing park and open space referendums with such comfortable margins that proposing them is beginning to appear a political necessity rather than a liability. An oft-cited example of the efficacy of civic involvement is in Huntington, Long Island, where a $2.5 million, 10-park package was first defeated and then passed after a "Citizens Action Committee" got behind the purchase. The vote was five to one in favor.

Still, there is a school of thought that insists the safer way is to buy lower price properties on short term bonds that don't require referendums. In the town of Cortlandt, in Westchester County's northwestern corner, a park program has been stalled on this very issue. Cortlandt, which is purely rural in spots, tightly packed in others, would seem to require several outdoor recreation sites distributed around its 33 square miles.

A Piecemeal Effort: Cortlandt

The process began in 1960 when a town councilman, William Michaelsen, began to realize the importance of outdoor recreational sites to the people of his town. Moreover, he was aware—and in those days it was a unique awareness in Cortlandt—that the town didn't have much time to get its recreational house in order. Cortlandt had noticed a slow-down in residential development although the decade of the fifties had seen thousands of acres of farmland swept under by housing developments in the town's north end. Michaelsen knew that it would start up again in the decade of the seventies. Proposing a tract bordering on Peekskill Hollow Brook—which runs sweet and full year-round—Michaelsen was opposed by an ambitious out-party candidate and his referendum went down to defeat amidst seamy implications of party favoritism and wheeling and dealing. Discouraged almost to the point of bitterness, Michaelsen remained on the town board but withdrew his neck on the recreation issue.

He surfaced again in 1965 when he found that his cautious probings for support on the board were eagerly endorsed by two new Councilmen, John Kelly and Gilbert Simonetti. The pair were from the town's minority party, but to Michaelsen's delight were not at all of the same stripe as his earlier antagonist. Michaelsen, Kelly and Simonetti quickly formed an *entente cordiale* as far as recreational land acquisition was concerned. When the opportunity to purchase a defunct 60 acre day camp arose, the trio, comprising a majority of the board, moved strongly for its acquisition. The price—a bit over $100,000—was affordable for short term bonding. The once-burned-twice-shy Michaelsen urged purchase without referendum.

Although the proposed site, Pine Lake Camp, had everything going for it, including support from both parties, dissident elements in the community managed to get up a petition to force the purchase to referendum. But Michaelsen persuaded his colleagues on the board to vote for the purchase without referendum anyway since the dissidents were politically unimportant and since their petition had no legal force. Pine Lake Camp became Pine Lake Park and work was begun on developing an old lake bed on the property into a swimming area.

Emboldened by his success, Michaelsen next went after a smaller piece in a less well-heeled section of town, the hamlet of Verplanck, which had been demanding recreational facilities for years. No referendum; no problem.

But Michaelsen's failure half a decade earlier still nagged at him. The populous north end was crawling with children, none of whom had so much as a place to swim. Recreation Director Matthew Dolan had pointed out that the demand for his department's programs—held largely on school grounds—was at twice the rate there than anywhere else in the town. Now that the idea of acquisition had some momentum and since he had staunch allies in Kelly and Simonetti, he figured the time was ripe for another assault on his first project. The land that bordered Peekskill Hollow Brook was still available although the price had gone up. But Michaelsen was able to persuade the town board to

vote unanimously to begin negotiations with the owner and

to move quickly toward short term bonding once the final price had been agreed on.

Hardly had these intentions been recorded than a new group formed which, like the earlier Pine Lake opponents, sought to force the board to submit the purchase to a referendum. The group, calling themselves the "Cortlandt Citizens for Good Government," was led by the owner of a nearby commercial recreation site. Nevertheless they garnered considerable membership among the disenchanted and disaffected throughout the town on the recreation issue as well as on other problems the board had been having. In no time, the CCGG began developing effective connections with the major political party.

On July 19, 1966, the group arrived in strength at the board meeting to submit a petition of some 900 names demanding that the board let the purchase go to referendum, despite the fact that the owner, having been humiliated once, swore to withdraw the property if such a thing came to pass. Confronted by considerable political power, Cortlandt's Supervisor, Charles Cook, moved to rescind the motion to purchase the property made a month before. Cook's motion failed three to two—the Michaelsen-Kelly-Simonetti alliance prevailing. Michaelsen then made a motion to "receive and file" the petition—thus giving it no status. This motion was carried, again three to two.

Predictably, the meeting, packed with outraged CCGG members, erupted into name-calling cacaphony. One CCGG leader yelled at Michaelsen, "You say you believe in the people and yet 1,000 of these people can go to hell!"

Replied the Councilman, "I intend to stick by my guns."

To his dismay, however, Bill Michaelsen found that sticking by his guns wasn't enough. When it came time to vote on the bonding, more than a simple majority was required. The CCGG had not let up on its attack and even began derogating the sites already acquired, calling Pine Lake "Pine Lake Swamp" and the Verplanck acquisition a "mudhole." The three-two division remained as a block to the issuance of serial bonds, which required a majority 31 of four. Michaelsen went down in flames for the second time over the same piece of property.

The CCGG, not satisfied with winning the battle, wanted its pound of flesh and set about to "get" Michaelsen as well as Kelly and Simonetti. They began a program of harassment so brutal that the Town Council finally had to pass a ruling severely limiting citizen participation at board meetings. In the elections of 1967, the CCGG sponsored a third party which so confused the electorate that while no CCGG member won a seat, John Kelly lost his to a candidate not willing to support Michaelsen's acquisition program in the manner to which he had become accustomed. With only Simonetti left to help, the current prospects for a purchase without referendum are so small as to be invisible.

Need for a Civic Base

Bill Michaelsen is one of the few martyrs of open space, but his story is just as instructive as the New Canaan victory, if not more so. There is no gainsaying the fact that a referendum now on the Peekskill Hollow Brook site might well be defeated, but this would be a superficial reading if applied to other communities. What Michaelsen lacked throughout was any kind of civic base for his effort. It is true that in the early sixties such a base might have been hard to come up with. But today, even in Cortlandt, it's much simpler. With such a base, such as New Canaan's Lloyd-Lapham Property Committee, the matter of referendum becomes an entirely different proposition, and certainly the scope of acquisition plans can be much enlarged from the piecemeal to the comprehensive.

Shifting Attitudes

In the case of Cortlandt, a town with several centers rather than one, a piecemeal effort probably would not succeed because one section of the town would be unwilling to buy a park for another section. A park "package" like Huntington's might well have been another matter, and some observers fault Michaelsen for not considering the possibility or trying to muster town-wide support for such a program. It is axiomatic that public attitudes concerning landscape protection and recreation have changed

32

markedly since the late fifties and the early sixties. Michaelsen, bloodied by a defeat during that period, assumed no shift in public attitudes in the intervening six years. While this analysis is wholly academic for Cortlandt, it has great relevance to other communities in the process of deciding how to program their acquisitions. The trouble with thinking small is that the result is small. Faced with viable community attitudes and with a limited time in which to act—from the point of view of land prices as well as sheer availability—many municipalities, like New Canaan, are beginning to undertake acquisition programs at levels unheard of ten years ago.

One further point should be made here: the project has to be sufficiently exciting to arouse civic support. The compelling nature of New Canaan's 300-acre proposal was lacking in Cortlandt's chunk by chunk approach. The Lloyd-Lapham plan engaged the imagination of New Canaan's civic leadership. It became a *cause* for the community's influentials. In Cortlandt, where there are just as many boards and commissions and civic groups, the threshhold of civic engagement was nowhere in sight. The Cortlandt Conservation Association, for example, in spite of its 400 member strength, limited its support of the acquisitions to a single letter sent to the board.

Still, if Michaelsen was not altogether successful, his contribution was great—both in terms of open space preserved, as well as in terms of providing an instructive case history. His odyssey points up the need for careful, up-to-date political analysis as well as contemporary political courage. In Michaelsen's case, if there was some question about the first, there was certainly none about the second.

One of the significant factors in the shifting attitudes concerning the landscape and outdoor recreation has been the potpourri of State and Federal grant programs. As any discount house merchandiser will testify, Americans like a bargain, even if it is only the possibility of one. By and large this is the most important effect governmental grant programs have had on municipalities. The actual money

Grant Programs

has been relatively thin, but the possibility of bargain has been great enough to get many a municipality into the store.

Nevertheless, at this stage of the game, it is important that municipalities be very realistic about grants-in-aid for open space. A municipal official who promises a bargain to his electorate and comes home empty handed can find himself in a very delicate position.

Land and Water Conservation Fund

The fact of the matter is that currently most State and Federal programs are seriously oversubscribed. One example is the Federal Land and Water Conservation Fund administered through the states by the Bureau of Outdoor Recreation, an arm of the Department of the Interior. The grants can cover both acquisition and development on a fifty-fifty basis. The Fund derives its income from motor boat fuel taxes, revenues from National Parks and the sale of the Golden Eagle Passport, which is a kind of season ticket to National Parks and a fund-raising device. According to Edwin Shellenberger, Acting Chief of Grants-in-Aid, our of BOR's Philadelphia office, the total money requested by the states from the program's inception in 1965 in the Middle Atlantic and New England Area (which include the local projects channeled through state machinery) is $79,897,996. But only $56,276,033 has been allocated for this purpose. Actually, this $23 million deficit is misleading, since State officials do a good deal of initial screening, aware of the limitations of the Fund. Says Shellenberger, "Many States are not submitting because they realize BOR doesn't have the money." Even so, some are really putting on the pressure. New York, for example, has requested over $22,000,000, although only $12,000,000 has been allocated. There is no doubt that many municipal officials are or have been disappointed. One ray of hope on BOR's horizon are bills in Congress currently under discussion that would add Federal income derived largely from offshore oil and mineral leases to the Fund.

HUD's Open-Space Program

The other major Federal program is the Department of Housing and Urban Development's Open-Space Program.

This also provides a fifty-fifty match for acquisition but only minimal amount for development. Their emphasis is more on land than on recreational facilities and more on the processes of urban development. They differ, too, from the Land and Water Conservation Fund in that local governments make application directly rather than through the states.

For this reason, the Open-Space Program is more indicative of just how far applications for grants outreach the supply of money. HUD officials currently are in receipt of applications requesting a total of $128 million. So far they have approved $47.9 million in applications, but rejected $66.1 million; $14.3 million has been set aside for future deliberation.

In view of the increasing demands on the program, HUD officials have established a new "Funding Analysis System" for grant approval. The earlier first-come, first-served technique was obviously impossible to administer fairly and subjective grading of applications was too difficult and could lead to long delays.

What their new priority system reflects, according to Thomas S. Israel, Deputy Director of HUD's Division of Land Development, is considerably less emphasis on large tracts of land—such as golf courses far from areas of urban concentration—and more emphasis on lands that provide visual and recreational relief in areas of greater population density and in low income areas. For municipalities on the urban fringe HUD is more interested in their using innovative methods of open space preservation, such devices as long term options or less than fee acquisitions. They are actively encouraging municipalities with new ideas to get in touch.

An important result of the new criteria—especially for those municipal officials who have experienced the molasses-like administrative processes of the Department—is a significant speed-up in the reviewing of applications. Says Israel, "We hope to be able to say yes or no to local officials within three to four months."

State Aid In respect to major state aid programs, the money available to municipalities is also thinner and slower than officials and civic leaders would like. Indeed, many of the best bond issues are flat broke. Both New York with its $100 million open space bond and New Jersey's $60 million Green Acres money are for all intents and purposes exhausted. New York's Next Step Bond Issue of $200 million, which passed in 1966, provides some money for acquisition —mostly in the form of additions to existing parklands. But it is mainly concerned with development of the recreational facilities on the land purchased by the earlier $100 million.

All this is not to say that State and Federal government does not hold some potential in terms of grants-in-aid to localities, only that the purse is not as bulging as it should be for acquisition. Municipalities are learning that they should not make acquisition plans wholly contingent on State or Federal funds. They should, however, always try, for they may succeed—especially if the grant request is for some new technique in open space preservation. Also, the only way Federal and State officials can get more money is by demonstrating that they *need* more money.

Grantsmanship Grantsmanship will, in any case, survive if not prevail as a municipal pastime. There are a multiplicity of programs that may or may not relate to open space acquisition in a given community. In more or less rural areas, for example, the Department of Agriculture has a program called "Greenspan" which provides grants for municipal purchase of agricultural land, which, under the Cropland Adjustment Act, should be diverted to conservation or recreational purposes. Elsewhere in the Department of Agriculture, the municipal grantsman can learn about Public Law 566 which provides Federal Aid for the construction of small dams and allied recreational areas. If there's no business to be had at Agriculture, one can pop over to Commerce for a look at the open space possibilities under the Economic Development Planning Program, which can provide up to 75% of cost of parks and recreation projects in redevelopment

36

areas, depressed areas and large development regions. The Department of Defense and the Corps of Engineers might relate to small boat and harbor projects involving recreational sites. In fact, the local grantsman can discover that commanders of military installations within their jurisdictions can be approached for grants for outdoor recreational projects or other community facilities. At the Department of Health, Education and Welfare the grantsman will find Title III of the Elementary and Secondary Education Act which has been used in some localities to help establish outdoor teaching areas, which of course contribute to the overall open space total of the community. Back at HUD there are more opportunities besides the Open Space Program. There is an Urban Beautification Program, a Public Facilities Loan Program, and grants will even be made to cover the interest costs (for up to five years) of land purchased in advance of actual municipal need. Those who are really dedicated to grantsmanship might consider sending for a telephone book-sized publication put out by the Office of Economic Opportunity entitled "Catalogue of Federal Assistance Programs." This book offers 459 program descriptions in over 700 pages giving the nature and purpose of each program, general information as to those eligible for assistance, whom to contact for further information, an indication of the availability of publications which describe the program in more detail, and the agency which administers the program.

With such a proliferation of programs available to local government, many of which relate either directly or indirectly to land purchase for open space or recreation, it is no wonder that many localities have appointed their own liaison people to deal with Federal Aids. In Bergen County, for example, Mrs. Marion Kress has been appointed "Federal Aid Coordinator" to compile and correlate data for reference by County departments and by municipalities. As part of her duties she makes studies, surveys and reports, recommending the uses of Federal Aid funds for specific problem areas. That aspect of the job might be 37 called *creative* grantsmanship. And just as important, Mrs. Kress follows up on applications expediting matters where she can.

Assuming a municipal government can find its way through the maze—with or without a professional expediter—a very real problem remains in respect to the proper "positioning" of grant applications in carrying out an acquisition program. In view of the uncertainty of success as well as the considerable time involved, many municipalities have learned not to make acquisition plans contingent on grant approval, unless, of course, the financial picture is too grim to have it any other way. For most suburban communities this is not the case, and though grants should be looked into, and possibly even applied for, acquisitions should probably not stand or fall on this point. This philosophy is strongly implied in the ambitious acquisition program mounted by Westchester County. In a list of sequential steps the County officials take, investigation of grants-in-aid is number eight in a ten-step program, coming long after initial contact with owners, appraisals and other matters.

Westchester's Acquisition Procedure

In fact, Westchester's procedure might well be a model for other local governments to follow. The County has certainly distinguished itself in the quantity and quality of its open space acquisitions. There are surely few municipal governments who have as much experience in the process of acquisition, and the County has no doubt discovered most of the pitfalls. As County Executive Edwin Michaelian has put it, "Land acquisition is always a difficult and sensitive part of government action, both because of the substantial amounts of money that may be involved as well as the complicated nature of the dealings between citizens and their government. It is essential that all parties' interests be protected and that there not be the slightest question as to the propriety of the procedures to be followed."

Pointing out that Westchester County has acquired nearly 2,800 acres in the last decade at a cost of almost $5,000,000 (including, incidentally, $400,000 in State and

Federal Aid), Michaelian prepared this procedure based on a good deal of solid experience:

1. *Master plan* — The property in question should be in the previously issued open space plan and program of the County. Acquisition of lands shown in such plan, or of other lands which constitute an amendment thereto, shall be initiated by communications to the County Executive from both the Planning and the Parks, Recreation and Conservation Boards, setting forth the basis for recommending acquisition.

2. *Executive review* — After receipt of recommendations from Planning and Parks, Recreation and Conservation (both staff and Board), the matter is to be discussed with potentially affected County agencies, notably Public Works and Law, under the initiation of the Executive Officer.

3. *Appraisals* — After staff concurrence, the Executive Officer is to arrange via the Law Department to have proposals for the necessary appraisals received from one or more properly qualified appraisers in Westchester County. Recommendations will be made to the County Executive as to the appraiser and terms. The County Executive will request authorization from the Board of Acquisition and Contract to secure the appraisals.

4. *Contact with owners* — After receipt of the appraisals, the Executive Officer is to contact the key property owner involved, advise him of the County's interest in acquisition, and request that he inform the County of the land's availability and asking terms for conveyance. ("Key property" refers generally to the largest parcel or the one that is most strategically situated in terms of the necessity for its acquisition or the one whose price would likely set the cost level for the remainder of the area.)

5. *Owner's agents* — Contacts shall be solely with the owners of property or their designated representatives (whether attorneys or brokers), and the latter shall in no case be dealt with except after they have produced a letter of authorization from the owner. The County will employ no brokers.

6. *Negotiations* — Negotiations shall be preliminary in nature, and shall not result in divulging the County's appraisal. No commitments may be given, though informal negotiations may be undertaken at a level as much as 15% in excess of appraisals, subject to the judgment of the County's representatives under the chairmanship of the Executive Officer. The County Executive shall be kept informed throughout, and wherever possible the prospective sellers shall be asked to submit or confirm offers in writing.

7. *Authorization by Board* — During the course of negotiations, or prior to it if considered appropriate, the County Executive will send a message to the Board of Supervisors seeking authorization for the acquisition. Such message shall incorporate the staff and Advisory Board findings as well as indicate the purpose and importance of the proposed acquisition. Information on maximum estimated cost may be supplied to the Board, with due recognition to the necessity to protect the County's ability to negotiate a final price. Wherever feasible, authorization shall be requested for an overall area described by its outer boundaries, with some indication as to the criteria to govern acquisition of individual properties; in general, the County will avoid acquisition of small properties that have dwellings. As requested, the Commissioners of Planning and of Parks, Recreation and Conservation will provide background information for the Board's Committees to which the matter is referred.

8. *Federal and State Aid* — Where applicable and appropriate the County will request Federal and State aid, and request for authorization to apply for such aid may be incorporated in the County Executive's message. After Board approval, the Planning Department shall prepare the necessary application and documentation forms.

9. *Acquisition* — After Board approval of acquisition and after successful negotiations, the County Executive will recommend to the Board of Acquisition and Contract acquisition in accordance with the nego-

tiated terms, as submitted in writing to the County. The Law Department will prepare the necessary papers. Where negotiation proves impossible, the County Executive may request acquisition by condemnation, to be authorized by the Board of Acquisition and Contract.

10. Finance and Records — A continuous record and inventory of all negotiations and related authorizations will be maintained by the Executive Officer, who shall at all times keep the County Executive informed. As required, the Executive Officer will request the Budget Director and the Commissioner of Finance for information on the availability of funds (including funds which have been appropriated but not financed) to cover the properties involved. As required, the Executive Officer shall keep the Budget Director and the Commissioner of Finance informed concerning authorization wherein funds are obligated, in order to control the availability of funds and/or cash flow.

The foregoing covers the vast majority of cases that will be (and have been) encountered by the County. Variations from this procedure may occur as a result of special circumstances—such as negotiations initiated by property owners, or opportunities for philanthropy.

While smaller governments might not have the breadth of staff indicated in Michaelian's procedure, the required functions can easily be assigned and the essential points of the process adapted.

One problem that remains in respect to direct acquisition is the possibility that an ambitious bond issue (with or without aid from higher levels of government) can put borrowing capacity dangerously close to the limit. Moreover, once a municipality has purchased what it believes to be adequate recreation space, it is hard to return to the municipal treasury for the purchase of land that has—at least on the surface—less popular appeal.

Two recent cases illustrate how this difficulty can be overcome by a combination of private financial grants and

Private Grants

short term municipal bonding or outright use of available funds. In Yorktown, New York, a 125-acre tract on Turkey Mountain—a major landmark of the town—was purchased via the help of two local philanthropists who put up half the funds. This was sufficient inducement—the municipal share amounted to only $30,000—for the town fathers to act with the assurance that tax payers could find no fault in their decision.

In another instance, involving land of a much higher per-acre value, 125 local contributors in the town of Greenwich, Connecticut, put up $18,000 so that the municipality could see its way clear for the purchase of four acres along the lower Mianus River. The total cost was $33,500.

It would seem that citizens—both those with modest as well as considerable means—seeing the effects of rampant urbanization, are now more willing to help municipal government in the purchase of open space as a means to protect the environment. Municipalities should, however, realize that the open space for which private funds can be enlisted is that which seems important to those who are putting up the money. Thus, municipal officials cannot expect private grants-in-aid unless the property is near to or beloved by people in a position to give.

While private grants can powerfully augment a municipal acquisition program—as can governmental grants-in-aid—they should not be allowed to delay an acquisition plan. There is simply no substitute for decisive municipal action. With or without financial assistance, direct acquisition must be an immediate effort in open space preservation at the local level.

Chapter IV.

Open Space and Subdivision

This chapter deals with the reconciliation of apparent opposites: subdivision and open space. The basic form of urban sprawl has been, and no doubt will continue to be, residential subdivision. The causes for this are several but not the least of them is the minimum lot size requirement levied by most suburban municipalities. In its day, this kind of requirement was necessary and valid, but most planners now agree that its day has passed.

There was an era when houses were built one at a time and contained everyone from Grandpa to the new baby. Since the end of World War II, residential development has been more of an assembly line operation than the application of old world craftsmanship. As a result, instead of the excitement of a new house going up on the block that many remember from their pre-war childhood, there is the disaster of a new fifty house development destroying the landscape. When zoning regulations geared for one-at-a-time construction are applied to fifty- or one hundred-at-a-time construction, open space disappears dramatically.

The contemporary answer to this dilemma is found in that misnamed, misunderstood and misapplied concept called cluster development. Basically clustering is a conservation measure, as much so as selective cutting or strip planting. It is not necessarily a method to enrich builders; it does not necessarily involve greater concentrations of people; it does not necessarily change the composition of the community; it does not necessarily put any more demand on municipal services. It *does*, necessarily, result in one very important thing: it saves land. The idea is perfectly simple: keep the density the same but plan on a site basis rather than on a lot basis in order to preserve a natural setting and maintain open space for recreational and other purposes.

Clustering as a Conservation Measure

The idea hardly needs to be justified here in respect to

43

concept. Architects are for it, conservationists are for it, planners are for it, consumers are for it, the Federal Government is for it, the National Association of Home Builders is for it, and probably most municipal officials are for it. Then why are there so few bona fide cluster developments in the New York region?

There are several score developments that have used a cluster type ordinance to achieve variations in site planning—for school grounds, for buffers, for minor open space areas, to fob off useless land to a municipality or a homeowners' group. But these don't count. If open space communities are a conservation measure, this aspect should be evident in the site plans: significant open space is preserved; significant visual amenity as compared to an ordinary plan, is created; needed recreational opportunities are provided.

The important thing about clustering is not to rehash the philosophy, to which most are already committed, but to get down to the basics of application. When cluster planning leaves the area of talk and arrives at the gates of action some real problems emerge. How can the citizens be convinced this isn't down-zoning? Won't clustering give the *appearance* of increased density, even if open space is saved? And how do you arrive at density anyway? Do you give credit for unbuildable land? If it's so good for the town, why are developers promoting it so hard? How do you overcome the popular belief that hard and fast minimum lot size standards will discourage development? Won't clustering *attract* more developers to the town? Who is going to take care of the open space? Won't it just be another dumping spot? How do you know that the open space won't be developed later?

It is these questions—or questions like them—that are the reason municipalities have approached clustering so gingerly. In fact, Hillsborough, New Jersey, which gained national prominence by permitting a cluster development, had a political upheaval shortly thereafter and the bars were clanked down again. Recently they have been raised to provide for a twenty per cent reduction in lot sizes if developers will cooperate in a "block development plan" developed by the municipal planners.

Dean K. Boorman, who has accumulated an enviable reputation as a creative planner along with his partner Peter Dorram, was largely responsible for the first step back to true cluster development in Hillsborough.* His answer is quite relevant for municipal governments that believe that out and out cluster planning would be politically impossible to introduce in one large step but would prefer a more cautious approach.

"Block Plan" Technique

Boorman describes it this way in *Jersey Plans:*

> Hillsborough Township, Somerset County's largest community in area (54 square miles of highly buildable farmland rapidly being developed), achieved Statewide notice in 1962 upon receiving the New Jersey Federation of Planning Officials' award for subdivision design. The subject of the award, Village Green, was and still is the outstanding example in New Jersey of "cluster development"—an area of one-family-per-acre zoning with the houses built on one-third acre lots and 40 per cent of the total tract dedicated for public parks and open space.
>
> Hillsborough's zoning changed and prevented further Village Greens. However, the idea of reserving open space and achieving better subdivision design was not abandoned. In early 1965, under a new Master Plan program, a greatly expanded new Subdivision Ordinance was adopted containing a number of pioneering features related not only to cluster development but also to a series of other aspects of subdivision design.
>
> The new ordinance was aimed at a series of problems in Hillsborough which are familiar to many of New Jersey's developing suburban areas.
>
> 1. *Problem.* Street layouts in new subdivisions which were being designed according to the shape of the farms being subdivided made no sense when put together into blocks.
>
> *Answer.* The new ordinance requires that every

* See Appendix F for Current Hillsborough Ordinance.

new subdivision must fit into a Block Plan (in Hillsborough, "blocks" between present Township roads are a square mile or more in size). The Planning Board, through its planning consultants and in cooperation with the developers, prepares the Block Plans *in advance*. The cost is made up by subdivision application fees.

2. *Problem.* No provisions were being made for school sites, parks and playgrounds and land for other public facilities.

Answer. A modified "cluster" provision, although not as extensive as in Village Green, requires the reservation of a minimum of 20% of the net site area for "Community Facilities Areas." These areas can be dedicated to the Township where appropriate—a school site and several parks have already been obtained by the Township at no cost but *only* where the Township wants the land. Otherwise, the open space is to be permanently maintained by neighborhood associations established by deed provisions, or turned over to churches or other semi-public institutions serving the neighborhood. The developers are allowed a 20% corresponding reduction in lot size below the former one-acre standard. This reservation of open space also helps in better street planning. The designer is freed from the usual necessity of forcing the streets into unnatural patterns following property lines in order to use the entire site for building lots.

3. *Problem.* Natural features such as streams, groves of trees, and hilltops with views were giving way to the bulldozer.

Answer. The required 20% reservation of open space allows preservation of most natural features. More than 20% may be required where, for example, U.S. Soil Conservation Service maps show flood plains or wet soil not suitable for building. These maps, prepared as part of a soil survey of Somerset County, show information of subsurface conditions not available from the normal topographic maps furnished by developers and have been extremely useful. Soil Conservation Service officers have also been helpful in advising on sites for ponds, which are valuable for drainage control as well as recreation.

Boorman would probably agree that the Hillsborough ordinance does not take advantage of the possibilities of clustering as much as it could—particularly in respect to open space. But it must be remembered that this is a community so frightened by development that its capacity for less stringent regulations is severely limited.

Another community battered and scarred by the bulldozers during the late fifties and early sixties is Yorktown, New York, where former Supervisor John Kibbe and his colleagues spent over eighteen months studying cluster planning. They drafted several ordinances before they were satisfied with the results.

One-Step Reduction Technique

The Yorktown clustering ordinance* goes a step beyond Hillsborough in terms of freeing-up the creative juices of site planners and saving open space. Their standards provide for treating an R-40 zone as if it were an R-20 zone, and pooling the remaining open space. They also say the developer can treat an R-20 zone as if it were an R-10 zone. In both cases, a tract of at least twenty acres is required. This allows a bit more freedom in design, however, than other clustering standards around the region.

Mandating Cluster

One of the most aggressive clustering ordinances (mentioned in Chapter I and reprinted in Appendix C) is found in the Town of Ramapo, New York. While New York law (Section 281, General Municipal Law†) says that clustering is not obligatory for either the builder or the municipality, the new Ramapo ordinance clearly states that "the Town Board has determined to empower the Planning Board to mandate the use of Density Zoning for a subdivision plat whether or not the applicant has consented to the use of Density Zoning." The degree of clustering permitted under the Ramapo ordinance is found in this paragraph: "In no event shall the minimum plot area of

* See Appendix G.
† See Appendix H.

any plot in an RR-80, RR-50, R-40, R-35 or R-25 zoning district be reduced below 15,000 square feet nor shall minimum plot width be reduced to less than 90 feet. In an R-15 Zoning District the minimum plot area shall be 12,000 square feet and the minimum plot width 75 feet. The land reserved by the Planning Board need not be all contiguous but may consist of one large parcel or strips of land lying between lots shown on the subdivision plat or any other design or location as in the Planning Board's judgment shall encourage the most appropriate use of the land."

These then—the ordinances of Yorktown, Hillsborough and Ramapo—represent three different approaches to cluster development. It would appear that at least a few governments are willing to grapple meaningfully with the problem of open space and subdivision design.

It is equally clear that municipal governments feel they must move carefully even to take that first step toward clustering. In Middletown, New Jersey, a "hot corner" of the metropolitan region as far as development is concerned, people inside the government are pretty well convinced that clustering is probably a part of the environmental answer. Thomas J. Lynch, a Middletown Planning Board member and former Chairman, points out that clustering would obviously be much better "than the type of developments that we're about to be choked by under the present zoning ordinances." At the same time, Lynch concedes this: "We're realists, too, and we know that the minute we mention clustering, we're going to be accused of zoning for particular developers or accused of downzoning."

Thus does the message come bubbling to the surface. The slow acceptance of clustering is not because of a faulty concept or even because there are mechanical difficulties in administering density zoning as opposed to minimum lot size zoning. The problem seems to be political; it is based on the fear that the purpose of cluster development will be misunderstood by the public at large.

48   But deliberate speed is called for, and the combined ex-

periences, both negative and positive, of the few communities that have successfully introduced clustering, can serve as a guide for the rest.

An important problem in introducing cluster is one of nomenclature. Whoever invented the term "cluster development" should get an F in public relations because image-wise it connotes, in William H. Whyte's phrase, "the doughnut rather than the hole." The hole is what municipal officials and their constituents are interested in. This message has not been lost on the builders either. Recently, the National Association of Home Builders, recognizing which side of the bread the PR butter ought to be on, has started to call the device "open space communities." This is getting closer to the bone, but still the term can lead to confusion, since "open space" has traditional semantic implications that range beyond a type of development. One Madison Avenue operative has suggested "green space developments" as an alternative providing the most precise nomenclature. It is, however, offered here without much hope that it will be adopted. This is too bad, because as long as "green space developments" are called "clustering," the typical uninformed response will be: "Clustering? You mean houses all pushed together? That's what I've been trying to get away from. Doesn't sound like a very good idea to me."

A Question of Nomenclature

Another problem is one of source. Who's pushing these "green space developments?" The builders are pushing them, that's who, which may seem to some segments of the community like Jack the Ripper giving a testimonial for stainless steel razor blades. Many builders no longer deserve the disrepute they fell into during the post-war period, but the fact remains that they are as vulnerable to *ad hominen* attack as any group on the municipal scene.

Who Should Sponsor Clustering?

The people in Yorktown, to return to this example, have as much if not more right than nearly anybody in the metropolitan region to feel victimized by developers. As one of the few places in Northern Westchester County with flat land, the town saw nearly ten thousand acres of first-class farmland turned into rooftops in a single decade. Much of the town lies in the Lakeland School District: a huge school population and one of the lowest ratios of assessables to pupils in the State of New York.

Still, Yorktown has passed its cluster ordinance, and at the final hearing, there was but one protest—a mumbled "this seems like down-zoning to me."

One of the most important reasons the ordinance could receive support from the community was that it was *not* proposed by a builder, but by the officials themselves. Although builders had submitted plans involving clustering, they were not considered until the cluster ordinance was passed. Another part of the strategy lies in the important fact that cluster zoning was not brought up to the residents all by itself; it was part of an overall revision of the town's master plan. As Supervisor John Kibbe (now retired) puts it, "Psychologically it was a good time to bring it in, because there were many things in the plan to object to—not just the cluster provision. Their attack had to be scattered over a wide field." In Yorktown, then, the winning ticket as far as green space development is concerned was that the ordinance was not only set forth by the officials—a much better source than a developer who might stand to gain financially—but also that the ordinance was a *part* of an overall re-evaluation of planning policy. In this framework, through neighborhood meetings as well as hearings, the officials could show green space developments as an integral and essential part of coming-to-terms with future growth.

Setting Standards

Another question to be answered about green space residential planning is in the area of standards. Once the officials in Yorktown had been able to communicate what cluster development was and what it wasn't, the big objection was one of "suspicion." As Raymond Margles, the Town Attorney at the time, puts it, "The people were afraid a sneaky builder would come in and put one over on us stupid officials."

According to Margles, the way to stop this suspicion cold in its tracks is via standards. "The objection that I

50

heard time and time again," says Margles, "was that clustering would be, in effect, a down-zoning, a give away to builders. Developers would—or so the reasoning went— take a piece of property that was, say, buildable to the extent of 60%, concentrate his building area in that percentage of the land, and then give away the part that wasn't buildable—swamp, hills and so forth.

"Now," Margles goes on, "if this had been developed along the normal half-acre zoning standards, he would have been unable to build in the swamp or on the hill, and therefore, in effect—this was the theory—clustering would permit him to build more houses than he could under actual conditions just because he could show us X number of half-acre lots on a map, ignoring actual building conditions."

"The simple answer to that," states Margles, "lies in the standards. If what cluster zoning attempts is valid—and saving green space was never called into question—then it's only a question of protecting the municipality against unscrupulous builders by drawing the standards in such a way as to limit the number of houses to the amount normally buildable under existing engineering, geographic and topographic conditions—a determination that would be made each time by the planning board and other officials such as the town engineer and the planning consultant."

The Yorktown ordinance has a key paragraph which delivers the goods in no uncertain terms:

> The developer, at the time of application, will submit a preliminary subdivision layout conforming in all respects to a layout developed on a straight R1-20 or R1-40 basis, and having no lots smaller than 20,000 sq. ft. or 40,000 sq. ft. respectively. Such layout shall be reviewed by the Planning Board to ascertain compliance with the existing regulations and will be utilized to set the maximum number of dwelling units to be allowed by clustering. (Normally in one family residential subdivisions, slopes greater than 20% grade, or low, wet, marshy or swampy lands are not con-

sidered buildable lands and, therefore, will not be allowed in the computation for allowable number of dwelling units.)

Said Margles, recently, "Given the validity of the concept—which is, I think, unimpeachable—if the clustering standards are carefully drawn, I think most people would accept it."

The Yorktown standards were carefully drawn, and most people did accept it. Recently, citizens from a neighboring development have criticized a nearby cluster, on the presumption that the builder is getting away with more houses. But the planning board needn't weaken because the standards provide them with firm, defensible ground.

Permanence as an Issue

The next question centers on the unknowns surrounding the ownership, management, use and, importantly, *permanence* of the open space saved via clustering. While permanence may be an issue with those new to the idea of green space development, it is relatively easy to provide for it in a local ordinance such as Yorktown's ("The common open space(s) shall be shown on the subdivision plan and with appropriate notation of the face thereof that it shall not be used for future building lots") or in some others to provide for a covenant or negative easement running to the municipality, protecting the area in perpetuity against development.

But permanence takes on real meaning only when related to the use projected for the open land. Shall it be owned by the municipality and operated as a kind of public park? Or shall it belong to the developer or to a homeowners' association which he would set up?

Who Should Own the Open Space?

These are not idle philosophical arguments at all. Uncared for, unused open space can have as many liabilities as assets. And one of the most important liabilities is the likelihood that no matter what legal strings may be attached to such a chunk of land, if it is not valued as green space by the next generation—or even ten years hence—it is only a matter of time before it *will* be built upon.

In New Jersey, and in a few New York State municipalities, the tendency seems to be toward municipal ownership and maintenance of open space derived through clustering. The proponents of this method cite permanence, capability for recreation development, as well as for continual maintenance and community-wide usefulness in support of governmental ownership. The open spaces in the Hillsborough development, Village Green, are owned and operated by the township, and the land is used by residents throughout the town, specifically for the Little League.

Many planning professionals and builders believe this to be a poor idea—first, from the standpoint that green space development might very well be arbitrarily limited by the amount of park acreage the community would be able to service and use, and second, from a kind of philosophical view. The people to whom the open space belongs are those who paid for it. When the developer sells a house, he is passing along, and making a profit on, all of his costs including that of the raw land to begin with. Therefore, the rights to the open space belong logically to the buyers of the houses.

The way to keep such lands maintained and out of the refuse dump category, say the professionals, is to establish a homeowners' association, in which membership would be mandatory for the buyers, with the stipulation in the deeds that the homeowners will be assessed pro rata the cost of maintaining the land as a recreational area. This would be accomplished via covenants, and those who defaulted on payment of the assessment would have this sum placed as a lien on their property.

The municipal-ownership people come back at this with the rejoinder that a lien is a serious but not very effective or speedy way to extract money from recalcitrant homeowners if the open space is being abused or uncared for.

Lately, an idea has been emerging which promises to provide the best of both worlds: the permanence and solidity of municipal stewardship as well as the rights of the buyers freely to enjoy that which they have paid for.   53

The compromise comes in the form of a special park district coterminous with the development. It can be set up upon plat approval to reinforce a homeowners' association. This way there is no question about getting the maintenance money out of the homeowners, for the municipality's power to tax can be used in the event that the homeowners' association becomes defunct. At the same time the entire cost of development and maintenance is borne by the people using the land.

Will Clustering Stimulate Development? Another question: will a density zoning ordinance permitting green space communities attract builders? The officials in Hillsborough would certainly agree. This attraction was the main reason they rescinded the ordinance that allowed Village Green. On the other hand, an official of nearby Middletown has said wryly, "we've *never* had any trouble attracting developers." Perhaps this is closer to the truth of the matter. Even with Hillsborough's ordinance amended to provide the minimum 20% reduction allowance, the township, according to Planning Board Chairman Mark Singley, has 2,000 approved lots, still unbuilt on, with more applications coming in every day. This is perhaps a prize-winning scary statistic for exurban New Jersey, but hardly a novel predicament for closer-in suburbs, cluster zoning or not.

The moral is plain. There is hardly an area within fifty miles of Times Square that won't reach and probably exceed its zoned capacity in fifteen or twenty years. Since green space development doesn't change this capacity, trading the environmental quality that can be gained through this kind of zoning for a handful of years doesn't seem like much of a bargain.

The final question relates to this very point. Isn't it possible that an ordinary, uninspired green space development will be just as depressing as the ordinary, uninspired grid or curvilinear development that it seeks to improve upon?

This has been one of the criticisms levelled against many cluster developments. The argument can be dismissed, of course, by the observation that without the open space

54

preserved they would have been worse. But this is an abrogation of the creative design potential available through green space residential planning. To the site planner that's the single most important justification of clustering.

Happily enough, municipalities have a fistful of high cards in the matter of design. Given the need to reduce construction costs, builders have flocked to the cluster camp with great enthusiasm and municipalities are, therefore, able to exercise greater control over green space development plans than they ever legitimately could under a standard minimum lot size zoning ordinance. It is important that they do so simply as a matter of self-protection as well. According to Orlindo Grossi, Dean of Pratt Institute's School of Architecture, "A lot of preposterous plans stamped with the holy seal "density development" are waved at planning boards. Too often they were inspired by greed and not good design."

The Question of Design

Grossi suggests that adoption of a density principle is not "carte blanche" for the developer. While clustering is an important step forward, it should be accompanied by design control through special design consultants (not necessarily the planning consultant) or panels augmenting planning bodies. These panels normally take the form of architectural boards of review, and include in their membership citizens who are professionals in the design field. They can play an important part in overseeing green space developments in the municipality.

Summing up, once it is agreed that green space development is a better answer to the dynamics of housing demand in suburbia than the present rigid ordinances, the problem becomes one of communication—selling the idea to the citizens and showing how the mechanics of operating a density zoning ordinance can guard against bad faith and poor design. The consensus of the experts and municipal officials familiar with clustering seems to be this:

Clustering Guidelines

1. Although "cluster development" may be an honest term, try calling it green space development or something along these lines.

2. Officials should propose it to the community. This is a job for those without a financial axe to grind.

3. Adopt strict standards, which, while permitting maximum freedom in design, expressly prohibit greater density than a given tract would be subject to under the standard zoning ordinance.

4. Establish permanence of the open space through legislation or easments running to the municipality, and *insure* permanence of maintenance through a provision for a park district either alone or as a back-up to a homeowners' association.

5. Don't worry about attracting new subdivisions. The municipality will get more applications than it wants whether green space development is provided for or not. The community's saturation point might be briefly delayed, but only at the cost of irremedial damage to the environment.

6. Insist on creative design and administer design standards through a consultant or an architectural board of review.

Green space residential planning is so important a subject that the inclination is to write about very little else* in an examination of ways to preserve open space. Certainly in sheer acreage it has to outrank any other method. If a municipality has, say, 10,000 acres of vacant land, as many outlying towns do, zoned on the average for one dwelling unit per acre, the potential open space acreage might be as much as 5,000 or perhaps even more, which at no cost to the community could provide recreational facilities of high quality and constitute a natural environment worth looking at and living in—not only for the newcomers, but for the municipality as a whole. The saturation point for the region and for any given municipality under present zoning is right around the corner, and a tract developed under a minimum lot size ordinance represents a positive loss of irretrievable open space.

56   * Many have; see Bibliography.

Chapter V.

Land Donation: Fee and Easement

In 1965, the Westchester County League of Women Voters did a study for the Open Space Action Institute on the ownership of open space in the County. They discovered that there were no less than 1,203 private owners of significant acreage. In built-up sections they didn't count any tracts of less than five acres, in middling-dense communities, ten acres was the cut-off, and for most of the northern part of the County, tracts of less than 20 acres were not considered significant. The amount: 74,208 acres—almost 116 square miles of open land. Subsequent research in other ring counties of the New York region suggests that the total land in the tri-state area might well be as much as three-quarters of a million acres in this kind of ownership.

These statistics tended to prove part of what the Open Space Action Institute wanted very much to believe: that in Westchester and in other counties throughout the region, ownership patterns had not changed so much from the palmy days of great estates in the countryside as some of the more down-at-the-mouth observers of urbanization had predicted.

The rest of what the Open Space Action Institute wanted to prove was that some of these owners could be prevailed upon to donate some of their land for open space purposes.

The Institute now has a landowner program throughout the metropolitan region as a permanent component of its activities. It has found that there are about 10,000 private owners of significant open land in the tri-state area, and many of these are potential donors of open space for recreation, conservation, education and a host of other uses compatible with keeping the land more or less in its natural state.

57

For example,* in Westchester a physician and his wife had spent nearly twenty years establishing an "outdoor museum" of native trees and shrubs on their thirty-five acres in the midst of rapidly growing suburbia. Their question to the Open Space Action Institute was simple and direct. How can this land be protected in perpetuity? The field executive assigned studied the land and determined through several conferences that the owners had a degree of philanthropic capability. But uncovering a recipient willing and able to take on the apparently onerous task of careful management was a different matter. After considerable investigation of various agencies, the field executive persuaded a nearby Audubon Society chapter to become the recipient, which it was delighted to do, given a modest endowment to cover out-of-pocket expenses for operation as a sanctuary. Working closely with the owners, a plan was devised that would convey the land in sections and would provide an endowment via a will. This arrangement seemed to fit best as far as over-all estate planning considerations were concerned, as well as from the standpoint of establishing, step by step, a nature education program on the land. The owners, who will continue to live on a portion of the tract, are participating in the planning. One spin-off effect of the transfer was to spark the interest of contiguous landowners eventually to convey some of their holdings in order to expand the sanctuary.

Not all landowners are prepared to provide endowments, although they may be in a position to donate some of their land for open space use. In such cases, a recipient must be found that is not only agreeable to the donor, but sound enough financially to assume the cost of management. Often, the most obvious recipient is the best.

In one case, a landowner had for some time wished to donate her land, but believed she could find no recipient to accept it on her terms. However, the O.S.A.I. field executive quickly found out that the town government would not

* See "The Stewardship Program," a pamphlet published by the
58   Institute.

only be willing, but was eager to have the land for outdoor recreation purposes and was fully prepared to establish programs on the property which were consistent with the landowner's interests.

The trick is, of course, to bring the landowner's interests in line with the interests of the community. There is some evidence that the trick can work. In 54 projects (averaging 100 acres apiece) the Open Space Action Institute has reported that over $2.0 million worth of land has been transferred under its Stewardship Program. Another $2.5 million is pending transfer and $6.0 million is in the "high potential" category.

For local officials not involved in these projects, the most important products of this work are the techniques established for dealing with estate owners.

The first lesson is not to limit municipal participation to the land offered to the municipality itself. The land that becomes a sanctuary owned by, say, the Audubon Society, the Nature Conservancy or a local "land trust" is just as valuable to the community at large as a municipal park. In fact, it's sometimes even better in a way, since the government bears no financial responsibility for development or maintenance, and in some cases, such areas continue to pay taxes or make a payment in lieu of taxes if they are tax-exempt. In the Town of North Castle, New York, for example, officials actively encouraged the transfer of the 120-acre, $650,000 estate of pulp and paper titan Louis B. Calder to Fordham University for a biological sciences study area. The land would be preserved and local residents would be welcome at certain times for fishing, hiking and nature study. Even with the loss of a sizable ratable, it would be, they figured, a much better and cheaper alternative than another housing development. As it turned out, North Castle could have its cake and eat it too. Fordham announced to the delighted town fathers that it would assume the burden of seeing to it that North Castle didn't lose any revenue from the transfer, even though Fordham was tax-exempt.

Using a Range of Recipients

59

The second lesson, which is a corollary of the first, is to recognize and respect the landowner's motives and self-interest. As for motive, it is a sad but true fact that most well-heeled landowners are highly suspicious of municipal government. Although this may be an ungenerous attitude, it's understandable that when a landowner is thinking about bestowing his greatest treasure on some worthy recipient, one of the last organizations he thinks of is the one which collects taxes from him.

Land Trusts
In Connecticut, where the municipal encouragement of land philanthropy is a higher art than in most other areas of the region, localities have formed quasi-official land trusts,* with self-perpetuating boards which are not subject to the political vicissitudes so feared by the landowner. Such trusts manage the land in the public interest, while respecting the wishes of the donor in operating policy. The land trusts have the support, if not gratitude, of the politicians.

**Conditions
and Restrictions**
Most landowners expect, and probably should receive, assurances that the public use of the land will be consistent with their image of it. It is the rare land philanthropist who thinks in terms of highly developed recreational areas, with ball fields, swings and the various paraphenalia of intensive use. Most of them would like the land to stay pretty much the way it is, at least for the foreseeable future. They are inclined therefore to donate land with conditions or restrictions, and to demand that the land be dedicated as open space so that it may not be turned by a future government or private organization to some other kind of use, such as a town gravel pit. This is part and parcel of their suspicion, and because they expect the worst, they try to defend their land against it. If a donation to a municipality is under discussion, the officials can usually make a deal if they are not offended by the implied aspersions to their constancy and if they keep in mind that a conditional gift is usually better than no gift at all.

In another aspect of motivation, many officials have

60   * See Appendix I for a typical land trust charter.

learned the hard way that the classical definition of philanthropy is not always what's behind a gift of open space. If for the Greeks it was "loving mankind," for the land-giver it's often just the opposite. In central New Jersey, for example, there's a wealthy lady most eager to give her land —500 acres in all—to almost anybody. The land is one of the most beautiful chunks of countryside in the region and sports a herd of deer numbering 50 head as well as full complements of other species. "I love the wildlife," she says with a soft gentility, "but I don't like people." She's perfectly willing to give the land away, just so long as no one is allowed on it.

Wildlife vs. People

Besides the spiritual there is also a financial motivation that defies the Greeks' definition of philanthropy. In one case, a landowner was in the midst of turning $100,000 worth of property over to an agency of a large city. In an intemperate moment, one of the members of this agency said, "Actually, all the old bastard wants is to get out of his taxes." Naturally, the comment finally reached the ears of the 'old bastard,' who thereupon decided he would be damned if he would give his property away.

Richard H. Pough, a naturalist who's an old hand at dealing with landowners, said of the incident, "Of course, he wants tax relief. That's what it's all about. Only an idiot would derogate this as a motive." Many landowners feel, and with some justification, that they've been giving their communities a free ride anyway by paying in taxes and receiving very little in services in return.

Financial Motivations

The financial motive relating to income as well as property taxes is probably a controlling one for most landowners, and well it might be. Under today's income tax provisions, allowing for five year carryovers, and the recent increase of the limit for many charities from 20 to 30% of adjusted gross income, there are not a few landowners who can come out on the plus side of things by giving land away. The landowner can, of course, take a deduction representing the current price of the land, as appraised. The fact that he may have bought it for $100 an acre 40 years ago doesn't mean a thing since no capital gains tax is involved.

Estate Planning   The third lesson municipal officials should learn is that a potential land philanthropist wants maximum flexibility in the making of his gift for estate planning purposes. Nassau County, which probably holds the record for complicated transfers in the New York region, can provide a good instance. The county worked out an arrangement whereby a large tract up for donation was divided into segments,* and then further divided into separate property *rights* that would be given. The plan was first to donate a positive easement over a large part of the land so that the County could establish a nature education program right away. Next, as the donor's income situation might dictate, full fee title on segments of the easemented property would be transferred. This could provide maximum flexibility in adjusting the level of philanthropy to income on a yearly basis. A deduction could be taken for the easement donation, which could if necessary be carried over for five years. Then as income changed or as other philanthropies might claim attention, fee simple transfers could be timed to keep deductions at an optimum level in any given year. A further wrinkle that was written into the deed was to permit the owner to participate in the planning process of turning the estate into a public nature education facility. Beyond this, there was a condition that the land would not be used for any other purpose than a nature sanctuary or similar use for fifty years, at which time it might, if conditions warranted, be turned into more intensive uses albeit remaining as open space in perpetuity.

From the experiences of those who have dealt seriously with landowners, it would seem that in most areas of the region municipalities can get a good deal more out of their landowners if they will expand their range to include encouraging donations to quasi-public organizations as well as to themselves. Moreover, they can especially succeed if they make an effort to understand the landowners' preju-

62   * See Appendix J for text of the agreement.

dices concerning ultimate use and his need for flexibility in estate planning, including the advantages of life estate.

Another form of donation is in the area of development rights. These are known also as conservation easements, open space easements, sometimes scenic easements, negative easements, conservation rights. A good part of the problem of understanding development rights is because of the variable nomenclature. Ramapo's "Development Easement Acquisition Law" mentioned in Chapter I, is yet another variant of the same thing.

Donation of Development Rights

Is a message imbedded here? The usefulness of development rights, *et al*, lies in their versatility as a tool for preserving open space which adapts to many objectives.

But perhaps it's best to go back to the beginning. Among the many accomplishments of author William H. Whyte (*The Organization Man* and others) was the popularization, beginning with an article in *Life* Magazine in 1958, of what he called "conservation easements." In this article Whyte suggested that a good deal more open land could be saved in the metropolitan countryside if governments would acquire some of the *rights* in the land instead of the land itself. This would mean that the farmer could go on farming, the estate owner could go on doing whatever estate owners do, and so forth. Governments didn't need to own the land to keep it open, they just needed to own the right to prohibit the owner from developing the land. The public benefit was conservation. The legal device is a negative easement. Hence, conservation easement.

If the majority of *Life* readers didn't rush to urge their elected representatives to get cracking on conservation easements, this wasn't the case at all with a small, but dedicated clan of conservation and planning professionals. Whyte's article and subsequent writings* on the subject were galvanic.

The trouble was that Whyte's apologists weren't as lucid as Whyte himself and they tended to oversimplify, so that eventually—and this is the case today—the idea of con-

* See Bibliography

servation easements became overly rigid. Municipal officials and others learned that you can't go knocking on an estate owner's door saying, "May I offer you a pittance for a conservation easement on your land, Madam?"

When Madam said, "Of course not, young man," or when Madam's lawyer, jowls aquiver said, "What the hell are you talking about?" the jig was up—or almost—for conservation easements.

Observes Nassau-Suffolk Planning Director Lee Koppelman: "In theory, the concept has tremendous appeal," and yet, "there are flaws in practice involving use and compensation."

The major flaw, as far as Koppelman is concerned, is this: "In Suffolk County—as in other urbanizing areas with substantial realty activity—the disparity in value of property for underdeveloped uses and its value based on the speculative potential when developed is tremendous. The sum that has to be expended for the purchase of development rights is tantamount to the purchase of the fee simple in many instances."

Koppelman, like most planners, is as good a student of political perils as he is of land use, and it may have occurred to him that the purchase of a conservation easement at roughly the same price as fee title for a piece of land might well be interpreted by the taxpayers as a case of not having your cake and not eating it either.

Thus did conservation easements fail to get off the ground. "I'm afraid," says Whyte, "the idea has been oversimplified. In order for conservation easements to be applied successfully, they cannot go against the grain of development—they have to be tailored to the topography. It is not a tool that can be used wholesale, particularly in urbanizing areas."

Gifts of Easements

When a gift of an easement is involved, the land in question must usually be relatively unbuildable and/or related to some important preservation purpose. In Litchfield, Connecticut, the Nature Conservancy, a private conservation agency, collected donations of covenants* from a dozen owners along the Bantam River. The covenants (in perpetuity) provided for the protection of a strip running two hundred feet back from the banks of the stream. One of the donors, an architect who presumably would know a thing or two about land values, said: "It *increases* the value of my land [emphasis supplied]. The river was one of the most important reasons for buying this particular piece of land, and anything that protects its natural state protects an asset of real value to me. I think it is also likely to be important to any future buyer."

In applying development rights as an acquisition tool, then, the municipality might profit from these conclusions:

1. Development rights, easements or covenants are simply legal agreements and can include a variety of prohibitions for the purpose of keeping open space open.

Guidelines for Easement Acquisition

2. Development rights make the most sense when applied to an overall program, such as the protection of a stream valley, or the protection of the natural environment surrounding or within view of an already existing public open space.
3. Development rights can more easily be acquired by gift than by purchase, if the land in question has speculative value.
4. When development rights are sought over large areas of buildable land, the chances are that term agreements rather than agreements which run with the land in perpetuity will be more acceptable.
5. The cost (or value deducted for income tax purposes) is the value of the land in its present use subtracted from the value of the land if sold for development as estimated by a qualified appraiser.
6. The assessment of land from which development rights have been severed should be reduced by an amount corresponding to the value of the development right. This is mandated in New York law, as well as being a basic principle of equal protection; it would apply in cases where assessment does not come under

* See Appendix K, L and M for this and other deed forms.

special legislation such as the Farmland Assessment Act in New Jersey or P.A. 490 in Connecticut, which provides for differential assessment.

Now that development rights, conservation easements or whatever, are beginning to gain respectability as they come into somewhat wider use, most observers including William H. Whyte himself are beginning to hope that the initial enthusiasm may not, after all, be very far off the mark. In suburbia, the chances are that easements can't be bought but they might readily be donated and along with fee simple philanthropic transfers can add a significant amount of land to the municipal total of preserved open space.

Chapter VI.

More Tricks in the Bag

The use of basic acquisition techniques having to do with purchase, green space development and the donation of land in fee or easement by no means exhausts the bag of tricks available to a municipality for the preservation of open space.

In Westport, Connecticut, for example, there is a zoning *"Design"* variation known as DDD. Like many municipalities anxious *Zoning* for a variety of ratables, particularly those low-slung, campus-type offices that never send children to school, Westport allows certain industrial and commercial uses if adaptable to residential zones. Westport's "Design Development District" permits these uses if they cover no more than 15% of the site and otherwise don't detract from the atmosphere of the town's pleasant residential districts.

This wrinkle in the zoning law was tailor-made for the Glendinning Companies, Inc., a Madison-Avenue-in-Suburbia type operation specializing in marketing consulting and promotion advice. (One of their accomplishments was the creation of Shell's Americana games. The idea has spread faster than virus X to most major companies that now have similar "games" of their own).

The Glendinning organization was bursting from its downtown Westport offices, which had no capacity for expansion. Casting about for likely land for a headquarters building, Bruce Glendinning (brother Ralph is President) found a 40-acre site in a residential zone (2-acre). The site already had one non-conforming commercial use, an embalming fluid factory which mixed its product in a two-century-old mill structure in surroundings of rare natural beauty, bordering a pond.

Luckily for the Glendinnings, the Westport tax structure and certain nature lovers, there was such a thing as DDD. Also luckily, the Glendinnings applied for a change of zone from the two acre zone to DDD in a way that brought all 67 their promotional genius, hitherto employed only in behalf of others, to bear on the civic structure of the community.

Armed with a complete dog and pony show of site plans and elevations depicting the office building proposed and how it would be disposed on the site, Bruce Glendinning and his associates collared everyone from the League of Women Voters to the near-neighbors. The climax of their presentation was a glorious full-color collage showing how the office building would look on the site, with precise indications of how the trees (photographed) would hide the structure (drawn). Then, just before the smart guys in the audience could start to say, "Yeah, but . . .," Glendinning flipped an acetate overlay, showing how the building would look in the *winter*—without the leaves on the trees. Says Glendinning, with obvious pride, "That little piece of work cost us five hundred dollars, but it was worth every penny."

There were still holdouts, of course, who fulminated against the plan principally on the grounds that it was (1) the commercial camel's nose into the residential tent generally and (2) what proof was there, specifically, that the 25-acre buffer area established in the application and in the regulation as untouchable really would remain unbuilt upon. After all, the reasoning went, the Glendinnings partially justified their commercial intrusion on the basis that a non-conforming use was already present on the tract. Why wouldn't someone else buy the vacant land and try the same ploy? Maybe, it was darkly hinted, the Glendinnings had this in mind all along and would promise anything, aware that when the pressure for ratables got intense enough, laws could be changed and agreements abrogated.

But it was not true. The Glendinnings were only interested in a good site for their headquarters. And as for the town officials, they were as interested in preserving the residential environment as anyone. In fact, they were convinced, as were most of their constituents, that the Glendinnings' plan for an office building would do more to preserve the feeling of countryside than a housing development—even on a two-acre minimum basis. But as the Glendinnings and the Town Planning and Zoning Board moved toward hearings, there was every indication that fur would fly and that possibly a court challenge to DDD might be mounted.

There it stood, until, in a surprise move, Ralph Glendinning announced that the Company would donate the 25 acres to a local, non-profit conservation body known as the Aspetuck Land Trust. The acreage could be put to use as a nature sanctuary. This solution (recommended originally by the Open Space Action Institute) did the trick. The opposition folded its tents (camel and all) and quietly stole away. At a final hearing, held in November, 1966, the League of Women Voters and other groups including the Conservation Commission and some of the neighbors, publicly supported the Glendinnings' application for a change in zone. The hearing should go down as some kind of record in the area of civility, good sense and capacity to put public purpose ahead of narrow self-interest. Even the lone dissenter of the evening had to admit that the plan was a good one. He could only warn the Westport Planning and Zoning Board that they shouldn't get carried away now with DDD because it might not always turn out so happily. From a philosophical point of view his observation was a good one. But for the moment, Westport officials and civic leaders could congratulate themselves on a solution that made manifest the fact that private and public purposes need not always be in conflict in respect to preserving open space.

The potential for commerce and industry to cooperate with muncipalities is rapidly increasing. Just to the south of Westport, Conservation Commission members in Greenwich are sitting down with the American Can Company to work out details for another office structure. They were most interested in the Glendinning-Westport solution. In New Jersey, where industrial development is as needed as it is common, many open space-producing sites are in evidence.

The key to civic suspicion does, however, if the West-port story is a guide, seem to turn on the permanence of the open space (as it does in cluster development to some extent). Where an Aspetuck Land Trust isn't handy, a good solution might be found in requiring that development rights on buffers produced in design development zones be granted to the municipality as a condition of certification, much in the same way that developers are required to dedicate public streets, or even recreation areas. The dedication of development rights would not require public access, of course, but would affirm perma-nence in the best possible way. The objectors to the Glen-dinning proposition were right about possible abrogation of agreements, and the rescission of laws. When develop-ment rights are held in trust by a municipality for the public there is much less chance that a future government can undo the good work of their open space-conscious predecessors.

This concept is offered, however, with full awareness that it's a seller's market as far as low-slung office build-ings are concerned. There aren't enough IBM's, American Can Companies, or even Glendinnings to go around. Plan-ners have been regularly chiding municipal officials about their impossible dreams of modern industry or laboratory or office building solving the crisis of environment. "Every municipal official," says one, "thinks he can establish a design zone and just wait for a buyer who will guarantee a building so low it can't be seen over a two foot hedge."

But a Glendinning should happen at least once to every municipal official, and very well might in this age of eco-nomic decentralization. When it does, it may present a good opportunity to save some significant open space while getting a ratable with no children to educate.

DDD and related ordinances found in many munici-palities are part of a larger category of zoning activity that can, as a residual benefit, produce a significant amount of open space. The category might be named "environmen-tal," and include all those real and dreamed of spearheads

70

of police power into the tangled jungle of private property rights. Flood plain and steep slope zoning are familiar examples, as are historic district zoning, scenic area zoning, and a practice that can only be called "extremely-large-lot," such as the ten acre zoning in New Jersey's Somerset Hills area.

There is a lulling quality about this litany, as if all a planning board had to do was decide what will and what will not be. The torpor can soon be torpedoed, however, by the courts. Flood plain zones in Connecticut, Pennsylvania and elsewhere have been found to be a taking without compensation and undue exercise of police power.

Professionals in the field of zoning law are quick to point out, however, that it all depends on the judge. Richard Babcock, a lawyer and planner, points out that in Pennsylvania, Supreme Court Justice Michael Mussmano could say this: "As a silk purse cannot be made from a sow's ear, so also a noisy, dust-laden, restless community does not become a residential, tree-shaded quiet haven through the instrumentality of a zoning ordinance." But in California, the State Supreme Court has declared, "If reasonable minds may differ, the ordinance will be sustained." Thus, says Babcock, in California, "it is possible to create a public beach by zoning property for use only as a 'beach'."

"Environmental" zoning thus becomes a process of municipal brinkmanship. Just as a Pennsylvania flood plain zone is struck down, so one is upheld in Massachusetts. In fact in the latter state it is possible to invoke the police power for the protection of salt marshes. According to Stuart DeBard, Executive Secretary of the Massachusetts Association of Conservation Commissions, the state can prohibit any filling or changing of marshland. If an owner feels he has been deprived of valuable rights he must prove it in court at his own expense.

Any discussion of zoning leads eventually into a discussion of taxing, and here the ground gets even mushier. Since World War II the cost of local government has in-

Tax Inducements

creased from a shade less than $8 billion to $46 billion in 1965, and will reach $108 billion by 1975. Most of this money—some 88%—comes from property tax. In many localities, increasing property taxes have had the tendency of encouraging the sale of land that might better be kept open, at least for a while. Recognizing that such increases might be causing premature development, many states have passed special legislation or amended their constitutions to permit a lower assessment on certain types of land. In New Jersey a constitutional amendment permits lower assessment of farmland (based on a table of values having to do with productivity)* with the proviso that if the farmer sells out to a developer, the forgiven taxes over the last two years fall due and the property returns to an *ad valorem* basis. In Connecticut, Public Act 490† states that farmland, forest and open space designated by the municipality will be assessed on "current uses without regard to neighborhood land use of a more intensive nature." Unlike New Jersey, Connecticut has no tax recapture feature. The State of New York studied these laws and others from Maryland, California and elsewhere, but has failed to enact similar legislation. In the opinion of one official of the Department of Audit and Control, Section 247 of the General Municipal Law is sufficient. This law permits easements, covenants and contracts with landowners and provides that assessor take such agreements into account.

Assessors like to juggle, which accounts for the low taxes on vacant land in many parts of the urban fringe. But they like to juggle on their own terms, and in Connecticut there has been a good deal of resistance to 490. In Middlefield, assessors refused to reduce the assessment on a private golf course which had been designated by the planning and zoning board as open space and therefore qualified for a reduction under the law. Among other things, the assessors pointed out that "it is not the intent of [490] to

* See Appendix N.
† See Appendix O.

72

benefit any individual or individual's financial situation."

Of course, the assessors were dead wrong, and the court told them so in its finding for the plaintiff: "On the contrary," wrote Court of Common Pleas Judge William L. Tierney, "the act clearly indicates that there would be financial benefits accruing to landowners, as an inducement to encourage the preservation of open space land for the purposes specified in said act."

This bears directly on the difficulty with preferential assessment as a means of preserving open space. True, it buys a little time. But there is no real contract involved as in an easement or covenant. Developments are still going up on former farmland in New Jersey and Connecticut in the same way that they are going up everywhere else. In fact, one of the results of low land taxes is speculation, which can have an effect that is completely opposite from what the proponents of preferential assessment want to achieve. Says *Nation's Cities Magazine* (March 1965): "In the suburbs, under-used land is taxed so lightly that prices have multiplied five, ten, and twenty-fold. . . . It is the primary cause of premature subdivision as builders leap-frog far out into the countryside to find land on which they can afford to build—often land that should be left open for years to come."

The suggested result, then, of reducing assessment is that real estate investors can move in and take a cheap ride while the land they are sitting on accrues in value. This may be open space while the sitting goes on, but most municipal officials feel about speculators the same way Benjamin Bunny feels about cats—you can never tell when they are going to pounce.

That there are so many different ways a municipality can preserve open space—and certainly not all of them have been recounted here—is probably of less importance than devising techniques that can work together. Isolated tracts of open space acquired one by one are a great deal better than no open space at all. But if all of the techniques for preservation can be used to supplement an acquisition

"Open Space Gestalt"

73

program, the land preserved can add to a more meaningful total, a kind of open space *gestalt*.

Take the case of Demarest, New Jersey. Over the years, the borough had come into possession of various parcels of land—some dating from the original land grant in the 17th century, others from tax foreclosures, still others purchased to round out a holding. By 1966, the borough owned 150 acres, which wasn't bad considering the fact that the total land area was a small 1,345 acres with a population of 5,300 which had increased twofold in the period of 1950 to 1960. The trouble was, taxes had taken a similar leap, and the time would not be far off when the typical homeowner would face a $1,000-a-year rap. Cost conscious citizens began eyeing the borough-owned open space, visualizing industrial and commercial ratables to help balance the tax base. There already was a pretty good sized town park—Wakelee Field—with 57 acres. Why not get some of the scattered chunks of open space on the tax rolls?

Why not, indeed. With an insouciance that could only happen in a tightly knit surburb like Demarest, the then mayor, Joseph Ringelstein, and his council sent out a questionnaire asking if borough residents would be pleased to have their taxes decreased by turning a 34-acre parcel into an office building or light manufacturing plant and turning an 18-acre parcel into a nursing home. An astounding 70% returned the questionnaire. But what really floored the Demarest Borough Council was that 50% said no, they would not be pleased to reduce taxes this way. At a subsequent hearing, residents attending made a strong plea for keeping these parcels as open space, and, in fact, criticized the council for copping out to "commercial interests." Ringelstein's rejoinder was that it was no such thing—the town fathers really wanted to know how the citizens felt. What came through, as Ringelstein put it, was that "people didn't want to sacrifice aesthetic value for a mere $250,000," which was the council's guess of what the two parcels were worth.

74

This story is instructive in two respects. For one thing, money isn't everything as far as the typical suburbanite is concerned. But more important—at least for the purposes of this chapter—is the fact that Demarest's open space wasn't pulling together, it wasn't additive, and was therefore surrounded with a good deal of confusion about what it was for and what to do with it. If open space is additive, citizens can see their open space whole, which they couldn't in Demarest.

During the midst of this perplexity, the borough officials asked the Open Space Action Institute to study the remaining open space in the community and to provide some kind of rational basis for decision making. An O.S.A.I. field executive set to work with the help of the new mayor, Adam Zaun, who took over after Joseph Ringelstein stepped down. After a careful inventory of the borough's landscape as well as demographic data supplied by borough planners, the Institute was able to see some emerging patterns and possibilities. The best way to control the environment of the community, O.S.A.I. concluded in its final report, was via the land still vacant in the borough. The land fell into three categories. First was the golf course, which might be protected by easement or at least be made to provide some breathing room by asking for a first-refusal agreement. Second—and this, the Institute felt, was the key——were the borough's undeveloped stream valleys. These were at once the major geographic feature, most significant amenity and because of drainage patterns in certain areas, most troublesome problem. In the third category was borough-owned land—more than two-thirds of the total—connected with these stream valleys. If the borough could control another 60 acres along the three major streams of the borough, an integrated open space system would be provided which could not only supply sites for outdoor recreation, but help control flooding and provide a web of natural land a short walk from every house in town.

The Demarest Open Space System

75

The borough needn't own all of the 60 acres. Trail rights-of-way could be set aside on one bank of a stream, but the other bank could be preserved via development rights either given to the municipality or purchased. On those properties which might someday be subdivided, average density zoning or cluster development could be used to free up the stream bank, and keep it in its natural state.

Certainly the O.S.A.I. report was not a unique perception. It was in no way revolutionary. Indeed, borough officials had already zoned the banks of the streams against development. But the report did show how the borough-owned open space could be increased in value to the community and it provided a backdrop for sound decision-making concerning privately-owned open land.

Mayor Zaun moved immediately by appointing a three man task force to refine and begin implementing some of the recommendations. Thus far, this group has persuaded the borough to purchase a small tract along one of the streams cited in the report and they have been working steadily with private owners. The most meaningful activity was precipitated by the requirement mandated by the State to begin planning on a comprehensive sewer project. For a while it seemed that the cost of this work might doom the open space program completely. But the Open Space Action Institute suggested that instead of invariably running the sewer trunks down the streets, the engineers might consider running some of them down the stream valleys and condemning an excess amount of land to accomodate the proposed walkway. Thus might two municipal benefits accrue rather than just one. At this writing the borough's open space task force is addressing itself to this idea with Federal and State officials.

The Borough of Demarest demonstrates on a small canvas how a variety of landsaving techniques could be used to preserve meaningful systems of open space as well as large important chunks. In contrast to Demarest, the Town of Pound Ridge is purely exurban with a total land area of 14,460 acres. Here, Town Councilman Fred Zwick set up a committee* to work with the multitude of large acreage landowners in the area. The instructions given to this committee: worry about getting the land first, and by what device and through which kind of ownership second. Zwick anticipates that some landowners will want to donate acres as private bird sanctuaries, others will be interested in conservation easements, still others in a method of development which can save valuable natural land. When it's all over, Zwick hopes that Pound Ridge will be festooned with garlands of open space which are interconnected, or as he calls it, "beads on a string."

The greater volume of open space that can result from using a variety of techniques is only achievable by municipal government acting both directly in its own behalf as well as urging private actions which contribute to the total effect.

In some cases, existing open space might serve as a starting point; in others, a geographical feature such as a stream valley, a ridge line, a waterfront. In every case, however, it is a foregone conclusion that there isn't enough money just to buy all the land that should be preserved. Moreover, every private landowner has his own axe to grind whether it's pure philanthropy or unalloyed greed. These two motives, which promise to be permanent, require that everything in the bag of tricks be used.

Using the Whole Bag of Tricks

Thus an open space system might be made up of such components as a cluster development, a town hall site, an Audubon sanctuary, a conservation easement, a sewer easement, a scenic easement along a country road, a trail right-of-way, an office complex, school grounds, buffer lands beside the A & P, plus, of course, recreation lands owned and operated by the municipality.

If this seems to some to be beyond the capacity of municipal influence, the only argument can be that at least a few municipal governments don't think so. It is most

* The original committee was later supplanted by an official Conservation Advisory Council.

certainly a creative kind of activity. It requires initiative. But just as zoning was once gingerly attempted as a means of controlling the physical environment, today the preservation of meaningful systems and large parcels of open space is now coming into use as the next logical step in coping with the inexorable forces of urbanization.

Chapter VII.
Economic Effects

The facts are pretty much in: preserved open space is the biggest land bargain since the King of England whacked up the eastern seaboard and gave it away to his friends three centuries ago.

These facts have to do with both negative and positive values based on two theorems: municipal costs increase with density, and municipal revenues increase with amenity. In both cases, open space can be the controlling factor.

A kind of "pop" suburban tax theory for conservationists was formally unveiled twelve years ago in a letter to the editor of the Lexington Massachusetts *Minute Man* (April 19, 1956). The author of the letter, Mr. Roland B. Greeley, at the time on the faculty of the Department of City and Regional Planning at MIT and a private planning consultant, probably had no idea how widely he would be quoted, or that for a large segment of the public he would become a prophet of what is now not so whimsically called the "new municipal math"—the truism that public service costs in suburbia increase faster than property tax income as vacant land is subdivided into single family developments.

The New
Municipal Math

Neo-bourbons and other exclusionist types have joined conservationists in a solid front of apologists for saving open space on the principle that it would save money. Mr. Greeley might admit to being a conservationist. The other labels should not be hung on him, a fact that becomes apparent only when his argument is reproduced whole, as it is here:

> To the Editor:
>
> There seems to be widespread concern about Lexington's rate of growth. I submit below the crude outlines of a process for restraining such growth I wish the Planning Board would consider seriously. Perhaps they already have; or perhaps they will wish to appoint a special committee to study the matter.

Most people come to Lexington because they like, among other things, its "rural atmosphere," its open lands and freedom from urban character. Most people who are now here are concerned about the rate at which that openness is disappearing. Such controls as 30,000 sq. ft. zoning obviously will not preserve the openness which we cherish.

Suppose the Town should decide to buy up, within the next few years, something like 2,000 acres of undeveloped land in the Town (the total area of the Town is about 10,000 acres), selecting the areas which are least accessible, least easy to service, least desirable for residence. What would be the result?

First, it would cost money—possibly a million dollars. However, unless the Town was forced to pay exorbitant prices for the land, the total cost, spread over a twenty year period, should not exceed $75,000 per year, including loss of tax income from the raw land.

Second, we would derive significant financial savings. Judging from post-war experiences, each new home pays on the order of $400 per year in taxes. If we assume that such homes average only 1-1½ school children per family, then the cost of schooling alone is equal to, or exceeds, the taxes paid during the first 15 or 20 years of the dwelling's existence. Thus the costs of school construction, sewers, drainage, street maintenance, and even some health and welfare expenses must all be met by the Town as a whole rather than by taxes on the individual properties concerned. Thus the net cost of servicing these new homes, if they are built, would add up to far more than the $75,000 per year which the Town might have to spend to avoid this cost.

Third, we would lose out to the extent of denying ourselves the addition of many new friends and neighbors such as those who have recently come to Town; and we might open ourselves up to the criticism of being "snobbish" or selfish. On the other hand, in the long run there may be two factors which will offset these arguments. The open spaces may, in their way, become just as great assets in the total Metropolitan area as such large open spaces as Middlesex Falls, Blue Hills and Breakheart Reservations are already proving to be. And the existence of such open spaces may, in the future, make it appear desirable to allow some residential areas in the Town to develop at somewhat higher densities, and thus more efficiently. If this proves to be the case, we could eventually absorb the same amount of additional growth, but at a slower rate and in a more economical and desirable pattern. If not, then we will be fortunate enough to have acted before it was too late.

Fourth, we would be guaranteeing the future existence of real open spaces throughout the Town—open spaces which need not be maintained (except for fire protection), but which would count significantly as far as amenity, appearance, and casual use are concerned; and which would count significantly, I believe, in maintaining sound property values in nearby residential areas. If, a generation hence, we find such land not to be an asset in public ownership, the chances are overwhelming that it could be disposed of at a profit. Personally I doubt if we would be willing to dispose of it at any price in the future.

If I interpret citizen attitudes correctly, a procedure of buying up open space reserves would obtain for nearly all of us the very pattern of development in the Town which we want most. And at the same time, for an initial expenditure of a million dollars (the cost of one school), we would have a very good chance of making a net profit (through reduction in Town expenses) of at least a quarter million dollars a year.

Roland B. Greeley

Although Lexington did not take Mr. Greeley up on his plan, he initiated a whole new way people could approach open space vis-a-vis the tax base. For example, the Princeton Township Citizens' Advisory Committee on Open Space (later made a commission) came out in 1962 with a proposal adding some significant detail to the economic theory of open space preservation.

Of greatest value to those outside Princeton, but never-   81 theless interested in its thinking, is an appendix containing some expert testimony on economics. It was here that Lyle Fitch, former Chief Administrator of the City of New York and now President of the Institute of Public Administration, gave Princeton officials and civic leaders some hard data to chew on. The service cost of new housing, Fitch estimated, would "be about $1,005 per household, requiring a dwelling and lot assessed at about $53,000" to break even on the tax base. The point hardly needs nailing down, for few communities can anticipate subdivision activity that will uniformly produce that kind of residential ratable.

The numbers produced by Greeley and Fitch merely quantify in a very particular way what is already known about the economics of development. As Fitch puts it, "The more densely settled an urban area, generally speaking, the lower will be the average value of each dwelling unit. The lower the dwelling unit value, the less its capacity to support public services. The cost of public services in urban residential communities, however, tends to increase with population density. Hence, greater densities tend to be accompanied by higher service costs per household, and lower value and taxable capacity per dwelling unit."

The Agent of Reversal: Open Space

That this tendency is not irreversible is the whole point that Greeley and Fitch were trying to make. The agent of reversal is open space. "There are cases," says Fitch, "where it will be financially advantageous to acquire land to preclude its residential development." And he has provided a somewhat whimsical formula for officials to follow in deciding between open space and subdivision:

$$I_a = \frac{C_s - (L_a\, t + L_f\, i)}{t}$$

I_a is the "point of indifference," the point at which the municipal coffers would be in the same shape whether a piece of land were developed or not. C_s is the cost of providing public services to the household, from which is subtracted L_a, any decrease in assessment because of, say, an open space easement, times t, the tax rate and L_f, the amount required to implement an open space policy involving purchase of fee or easements, times i, the interest rate on borrowed money for implementation. All of this is divided by t, the tax rate.

Fitch doesn't really expect anyone to work this out. He summarizes thus: "The township stands to gain by acquiring vacant lots or development rights thereto, rather than allowing them to be developed for residence, whenever (1) the cost of supplying public services to the prospective new households exceeds (2) the amount of real estate tax sacrificed by foregoing private development of the lots, *plus* (3) interest on the cost to the township of acquiring the lots or development rights thereto."

Actually, all that is needed to apply the "new municipal math" is a sharp pencil and an understanding of what it really costs to provide municipal services to new subdivisions. In Closter, New Jersey a controversy arose in 1965 over the acquisition of seven open space parcels totalling some 80 acres. According to an account in the Bergen Evening *Record*, Mayor James E. Carson applied a Fitch-like formula this way: If the land had not been acquired, 80 acres would accomodate 160 houses. The houses, if constructed, would produce about 200 children to be educated at an average cost of $720 for each pupil or a total cost per year of $144,000. Additional garbage collection would cost about $4,000 annually, additional police patrolling $6,000, additional fire hydrants, lighting and other services, $2,000, for a total of $156,000 per year in services.

Carson estimated the tax revenue to be $100,000 a year; therefore the community's net annual loss would be $56,000. The total cost of the property in Closter was estimated to be around half a million dollars. The borough has applied to State and Federal authorities for aid, some of which they have received. But even if they had to go it alone, the payout point would be something like a decade, after which the land would be pure profit, or nearly so if Closter stuck to its plan of limited recreation development.

Perhaps the most famous example, possibly because of

its presumed flabbergasting effect, was the cost study done in Lloyd Harbor, New York. When Robert Moses announced his intention to purchase the 1,426-acre Marshall Field Estate (now Caumsett State Park), area residents predictably enough complained about the land going off the tax rolls.

Responsive to the public mood, the village board hired a firm of planning consultants to assess exactly what the damage would be, and, yes, it would be significant—an increase of $2.58 per hundred, nearly 20% (from $14.33 to $16.91). But that was only a part of what the planners were asked to figure out. Assuming the land would eventually be developed, they set up a statistical model based on two-acre plots containing houses worth $35,000. In this case, said the planners to the dismay of some, the tax rate would go to $21.64, an increase nearly three times greater.

In spite of the persuasiveness of such statistics, it's important to understand their limitations. "Conservation is not contraception." said the late Hugh Pormeroy. The argument probably should not be used as an excuse for open space preservation but as a defense against the critics of acquisition. "I'm in favor of open space," they always say, "but we can't afford to remove the land from the tax rolls." *That's* the argument that doesn't wash, for 95% of the time, which is the incidence of vacant land zoned for single family residential purposes in the New York region, the greater loss to the community would be in *not* taking the land off the tax rolls.

Positive Results of Preservation A far more exciting phenomenon is the *positive* economic results of open space preservation. It is a phenomenon thoroughly understood by those who have the most to gain by it—the housing developers. What they know for a fact can serve equally well as an operating theory for a municipality concerned with the quality of its ratables.

Says Carl Norcross in his excellent study, *Open Space Communities in the Market Place*, if a developer "creates an outstanding environment, saves the trees, has a good street pattern, and then adds a pool and a modest recreation area, he might easily get $500 or $1,000 more per house than he would for the same house in an ordinary subdivision." This is, of course, a $500 or $1,000 that shows up on the tax rolls too. Norcross continues: "Proof that developers who tried open space and better land planning believe in them, is that in their next developments they have gone even farther to provide more open space, more recreation and better community facilities." If, as William H. Whyte has said, "Good aesthetics make good economics," that means they'll make a pretty good tax base too.

According to the American Society of Planning Officials (Newsletter, 1963, p. 92), it is common practice throughout the United States for FHA appraisers to place a higher valuation on houselots if the development contains a park or if it is adjacent to or near a public park. Moreover, according to the National Association of Home Builders (in Home Builders' Manual for Land Development, 1968), "Today's home buyer is looking for features beyond the confines of the house and lot. Proximity to school, park and community recreation is high on his list of looked-for items.

"This statement," continues the NAHB, "may not impress the newcomer in the building and subdivision field who has not experienced the keen competition of a buyer's market. The experienced developer, however, knows that the presence of these features enhances desirability, which is translated directly into buyer demand and sales value. *In the vicinity of park and recreation areas, enhanced values of building sites up 15 to 20%, with a high level of sustained value over the years, are not uncommon experiences.*" (Emphasis added.)

According to Dr. Kenneth D. Daane, who made these citations in an excellent study, *The Economic Implications of the Regional Parks System in Maricopa County* (Arizona State University, 1964, $1.75), "Public recreational facilities have significant effects upon the surrounding land and property values. In many cases the development of 85 park facilities has increased the values of surrounding realty to the point where the increase in tax revenue more than paid for the cost of the parks."

In a discussion of the economic effects of golf courses, Urban Land Institute Research Analyst G. H. Crabtree Jr. points out that these facilities confer two benefits. "The municipality gains substantial tax receipts from the surrounding property and has a spacious open green area in its jurisdiction."

In the city of Prescott, Arizona, Crabtree reports, the city built a golf course on land valued at $25 an acre. After that, city officials turned around and sold adjacent land to subdividers for an average of $2,277 per acre. "It is anticipated that the development of this land will add over $3,000,000 to the city's taxable values in the next ten years," according to city officials.

So confident of the value of large amounts of open space in a master plan, Wallace-McHarg, Philadelphia planners, showed a significant difference in development value in a comparison of optimum development versus a forecast of development patterns if present trends continued in the Green Spring and Worthington Valleys outside Baltimore. In their *Plan for the Valleys*, calling for preservation of 3,000 acres of meadowland, they state: "It has been calculated that uncontrolled residential growth develops approximately $33.5 million (in land value) by 1980, and Optimum Land Use residential development produces $40.5 million in the same period. The additional $7 million resulting from concentration would be adequate to pay in excess of $2,300 per acre for title to the 3,000 acres exempted from development."

What Wallace-McHarg projected and what Norcross observed in his study of developments throughout the country was a tangible improvement in property values because of open space. "Open space communities," states Norcross, "attract well-educated families, with better than average jobs and with middle or upper incomes. . . . A by-product of their education is an appreciation of an environment that will provide a better place in which their children can grow up."

An important by-product appreciated by many officials and civic leaders, is the direct effect of preserved open space on surrounding assessments.

To the people who wish to encourage open space preservation, these kinds of facts are tantalizing and they have been accumulating over the years. One of the most quoted is a before-and-after study undertaken by the Union County, New Jersey, Park Commission covering the period 1922 to 1939. The Commission reported a 631.7 per cent increase in the assessed valuation of properties within a quarter mile of their Warinanco Park, while assessments in the city as a whole (Elizabeth, New Jersey) averaged a 256.7 per cent increase.

Certainly if property value increases like this could be projected for any proposed park purpose, the people who come to town hall to militate against acquisition plans on economic grounds could have their arguments easily swept away. A more recent example can be found in Woodmere, New York, where Nassau County Assessor Horace Kramer has ruled that the 30- and 40-year-old houses adjacent to a golf course in this Long Island community are not eligible for reduction in assessment because of their age. "If these houses weren't in their present location," he says, "they would be entitled to a substantial reduction in assessment."

According to Kramer, this is perhaps the most important effect of open space—the maintenance and improvement of values over the long pull. "In Nassau we have the opportunity to preserve residential values by preserving open space. This increases the property tax yield which is the major source of revenue for local government."

It would obviously be a major breakthrough if a formula could project the effect of preserved open space with some accuracy. This way, pay-out points could be anticipated for a project that might, say, clear a blighted area for a park, counting on increasing assessments of surrounding properties to pay off the investment. According

87

to Harold Van Cott, Supervisor of Recreation for Essex County, New Jersey, this has happened in a way in the Brookdale Park area in Bloomfield and Montclair. The park was constructed during the Thirties in an area which had at least partially been blighted and could have deteriorated further. Van Cott believes that the park construction changed the direction of development.

Presuming that the most dramatic kind of persuasion is a good statistic, many open space advocates have embarked on a search for a method which could uncover this elusive economic grail. How much real estate value *is* added by open space, and under what circumstances?

Methods of Determining Positive Economic Effects

The closest anybody has come so far is found in a study undertaken by Robert L. Wonder for the Coro Foundation in San Francisco. The project got started in 1961 when William Penn Mott Jr., then Superintendent of Parks for Oakland, California, sent a letter to the Foundation stating the "need for concrete evidence to indicate that parks are good business and that the purchase of park lands for future use is good business for a city." One can be almost certain that Mott had suffered, as almost all park executives suffer, from simplistic economic arguments against parks. Robert Wonder arrived at the Coro Foundation as a 1964-65 intern in public affairs, and took up William Penn Mott's challenge.

Because so many things besides open space affect property values, Wonder searched out two parks in Oakland whose neighborhoods were more or less unaffected by wayward influences. A freeway, for example, might exert such an economic impact that the lesser effect of open space on land values would be virtually immeasurable. He then established "tiers" reflecting given distances from the park boundaries. The first tier were those blocks adjacent to the park; the second tier, one block away, and the third tier, two blocks away. If the parks had an influence on surrounding values, it would be proved, Wonder surmised, if these values decreased the further they were away from the park boundary.

Thereupon he looked up the assessments, block by block, to see if he was right. For one of the parks, Clinton, Wonder found that the mean assessment adjacent to the park was $3,416 and a block or two away considerably less. For tier two it was $2,300 and for tier three $2,355. Encouraged, he hurried to records covering the San Antonio Park neighborhood to make the same measurement. Here he found that the mean assessment was $1,489 for adjacent blocks and for two and three blocks away $940 and $1,006 respectively. Although these were two kinds of neighborhoods, Clinton Park with relatively high assessments and San Antonio Park with relatively low ones, the parks themselves did seem to affect the relative value of nearby properties. In the Clinton Park area, assessments were some 50% higher and in the San Antonio Park area 48% higher than other properties not so closely situated. That the per cent differences are so similar may be coincidental or may not.

But Robert Wonder had only begun to make his case. For the second area—San Antonio Park—he selected a control neighborhood which was the same as the "study" neighborhood in nearly every respect except that it didn't have San Antonio Park, or any park for that matter.

He divided the control area into three tiers, just like the San Antonio Park area, except that tier one was fronting on other houses rather than a park. Here, he found much smaller differences in the mean valuation of each tier, and of course no pattern. One tier was $876, another $932, and another $1,195, the greatest difference being 24%, and the overall value of the control area significantly less than the overall value of the San Antonio Park neighborhood.

With typical academic caution Wonder observes: "Because of the time limitations and the smallness of the sample it would be inappropriate to unequivocally state that this survey is conclusive in demonstrating that the presence of a park has an exacting influence on adjacent surrounding properties."

Then, throwing caution to the winds, he concludes, "Yet,

the survey does just that. Even with the smallness of the sampling and considering the randomness of the sample, this report demonstrates that parks do hold the value of their surrounding lands." He adds that based on a small amount of opinion research he did in park neighborhoods, "not only do parks influence assessed valuations, they also have an affect on how residents perceive their new neighborhoods and, consequently, a pride in the area is fostered by the presence of a park."

So far, two economic aspects of open space preservation have been dealt with: first, the penalties of not preserving open space in terms of the presumed alternative land-use, a single family housing development with two or three children per household to educate at somewhere between $500 and $1,000 per year each, and second, the positive values to open space that reflect themselves in assessments of surrounding property, if not in the municipality as a whole, stemming from the value added by the amenity.

Direct Revenues and Ratables
Another value is that which simply accrues *because* a tract is in an open space use, rather than in spite of it. This income can be either direct, as in the case of recreational fees, or indirect because of taxable values. One case illustrating the former is the improbable "Ski Bowl" in Brookhaven, Long Island, where 70 acres of land was turned over to the town via a density zoning scheme. Brookhaven is a town whose land area is bigger than most counties; its overall area is roughly the size of Nassau. Because it is big, Brookhaven officials can be forgiven for thinking big. The Ski Bowl was one such idea. Through the use of their "cash in lieu of" fund, collected from developers over the years who did not or could not make a contribution of land for recreational purposes, they were able to pay for construction. The project was not quite that simple; it involved a complex series of leases and the use of concessionaires. But the slopes and tows were built and a handsome ski lodge with snack bar and indoor recreation areas was constructed. How much does it cost to run the operation? Nothing. In fact, it makes money.

While certain open space uses are taxable, their taxation can often discourage the use itself, as the State of New Jersey found out when confronted with the massive pull-out of farmers in the Fifties and Sixties. Still, there are some resource uses that can and should remain viable economic assets. Outside of farming, other taxable open spaces might include forest lands for far-out areas, and closer in—on Long Island especially—marshland and shallow baybottom. Resource specialists have for years maintained that the most valuable land for food production is the estuarine marsh, comparing favorably with the most productive areas of the country's midland grain belt. When shell-fishing is involved, some interesting statistics emerge. Anthony Taormina, a biologist with the New York State Conservation Department, estimates that an acre of shell-fish rich baybottom on Long Island ought to be capitalized at no less than $4,200, based on a 5% factor since the resource is renewable year in and year out. With a good deal of justification, Taormina wonders why in the world people want to dredge these areas to convert baybottom to housing sites when doing so destroys such a valuable resource as the fancy-priced Long Island Bay scallop. The financial losses are additive: loss of a "cash crop," of amenity value to the community (most people would rather look out on a marsh than on the backyard of somebody else's house), the cost-revenue-formula-loss that obtains when vacant land is converted to single family housing. If you take Taormina's loss of $4,200, add to it a reduction of value of, say, 10% in surrounding assessments for houses that no longer look out over a marsh, add to this the net loss of tax revenue, subtracted from service requirements of two or three new houses, it makes some kind of total that indicates that a large amount of money has simply disappeared.

The point need not be belabored. Open space produces municipal income negatively—by costing less to service. It produces it positively by adding value to adjacent properties. It can produce income directly through user fees, or because a desirable open space use is also taxable.

The purpose of acquiring or encouraging the preservation of open space may not be a financial one, but acquisition is nearly always susceptible to financial justification. Indeed, there is so much evidence that open space pays off handsomely for the typical suburban community, that the objectors should be saddled with the burden of proof rather than the proponents. They are the ones caught with their tax rolls down.

Chapter VIII.

The Action Process

Recognizing that there is a preservation job to be done and that the job is financially defensible is the basis for action, but it is not action itself. For the work to begin, machinery has to be set in motion, and the municipal official and the civic leader might very well ask, "What machinery?"

In coping with the increasing forces of urbanization, the relevant departments of municipal government have become so over-burdened with the day-to-day work load that the requirements of tomorrow are simply beyond them. Suburban planning boards, for example, no longer do much basic planning thinking, if indeed they ever did any. They have been relegated to a semi-judiciary function involving whether or not the subdivision plat conforms with the subdivision regulations. They discuss the size of the pipe which will carry away the storm water, not the landscape principles that underlie a drainage problem, and certainly they are not discussing creative remedial measures. This is not because planners have no sensitivity. It is because they have no *time*.

Need for New Machinery

The recreation commission, too, seldom has time. Instead of being able to discuss the broad ramifications of land acquisition and overall recreation requirements, members become bogged down with the development and administration of program. Will there be enough buses for the senior citizen outing? Can we afford five more maintenance men this summer? How many parking spaces must we provide at the picnic grounds?

These are, of course, the nuts and bolts of government— to provide services, to enforce compliance with local ordinances. But who is in charge of tomorrow?

The answer lies in mobilizing and providing concrete direction to a civic element in the municipality which offers an untapped human resource of singular importance. These are the people already concerned about the natural

93

environment. While it is true that some of these individuals have been troublesome gadflies in their relationship to municipal government, experience has shown that given an official mandate, they will perform in the most responsible and seemly way, sensitive to the needs of the municipality in all its aspects, not just one.

New Official Groups This has certainly been the case in Massachusetts and Connecticut. In these states, and several others as well, enabling legislation has been set up for the establishment of "town conservation commissions." In Massachusetts,* where it all began more than ten years ago, most municipalities have such commissions. In Connecticut,* where the movement started a few years later, over half the towns have commissions. In New York State,* legislation was passed in 1967 enabling "Town Conservation Advisory Councils." While the idea was drawn from the New England states, the legislation is somewhat weaker and less specific. Even so, council formation is moving fast, especially in the Metropolitan Region where hardly a month passes that a new one isn't set up.

Conservation commissions and their ilk have been the most effective when they are peopled by citizen leaders with a demonstrated dedication to landscape preservation. This would include design professionals, such as landscape architects, as well as amateur naturalists and civic leaders with a proven capacity for "getting things done." In such cases, they provide an appropriate foil to the planning board and the recreation commissions, not a fragmentation of effort. This is because their focus is action, which is obviously complementary to the planning function rather than competitive. Moreover, their focus is on preservation of land for recreation, not the recreational program itself, which is the major job of the recreation commissions. In New England, recreation commissions and planning boards have therefore been strengthened by a good conservation commission rather than weakened.

All of this proves that the only way to get anything done

94   * See Appendix P, Q and R for Commission and Council legislation.

is to fix responsibility for it and to make that responsibility as specific as possible. In states such as New Jersey where no enabling legislation for local conservation or open space agencies exists, the capacity for fixing responsibility is not really any less. Some of the most effective groups have been *ad hoc* mayor's committees.

The first step in the action process, then, is to set up the *Initial Research* machinery. And unless a municipality has already done so, it should consider an entirely new kind of commission or board or council or committee such as enabling legislation now provides for in New York, Connecticut and Massachusetts. Such a unit should contain a heavy representation of existing non-official leadership in conservation, or more particularly in landscape preservation. And, importantly, it should be provided with adequate technical personnel. This means that the municipal engineer, attorney, planning consultant, recreation director and other professional employees of local government should be, if not ex officio members of the unit, then at least available to the group for consultation. Even better—and this has been done with great success in New England—is to overlap the various boards and commissions in their membership. This not only improves communication, but also eliminates the possibility of getting toes inadvertently tramped on.

Although setting up such a government unit is only a first step, it is in itself important, for suddenly, the elected officials have a built-in lobby for open space preservation *and* a wailing wall for the knotty problems of the environment. In both regards the conservation unit can serve as a political cushion. It can carry a politically difficult program to the general public and it can absorb the blows of a constituency outraged at unnecessary damage to the environment. It becomes a focus, therefore, both for action and reaction.

But for such a unit really to be effective, it must have a program. Unless it performs *work*, the council or commission is of very little account.

While conservation has many aspects that might prop-   95

erly fall under the purview of a commission, council or committee, it is likely that their main effort will center on landscape preservation, even if this were not the basic mandate in their formation. In this regard, there is a good deal of experience to draw from out of New England and elsewhere.

The first job is to find out where the open land *is*. This is mandated in the Massachusetts and Connecticut legislation. Elaborate inventories may be called for in certain kinds of landscape or ecological research. But for an action program all that's needed is to know who owns what and where it is. More detailed analysis can come later if required. To find out who owns what, one need only inspect the tax maps and the assessor's records. A serviceable list can be made of holdings of over a given amount—say five acres in close-in areas, up to ten or twenty in the exurbs —in a week's time or less by one or two individuals.

Ideally, this information should be mapped. The best way is to use USGS quadrangles pasted together to cover the entire municipality. (Rarely does one quadrangle suffice, except in the smaller towns.) Tax map information can then be roughed in directly on the quadrangles or on a mylar or acetate sheet, using roads and house locations as guides. If more accuracy seems desirable, tracings from the tax maps can be taken, reduced photographically to the same scale as the quadrangle, and then set up as an overlay.

The First Project   Once existing open space can be seen on a map, patterns begin to emerge. Moreover, by using the topographical quadrangles a sense of priority becomes evident, for these maps show both concentrations of population as well as natural features such as stream valleys and ridge areas. Rough estimates of flood plains and watersheds can also be determined and the existing open space resource seen in relation to the drainage patterns.

After the research and the mapping have been done, the possibility of an official conservation group dissolving into inaction is at its height because there is no end of confusion over what to do next. Experience has provided an absolutely clear, ringing answer: to identify the most important natural area on the map (or group of natural areas) based on the multiple criteria of amenity, recreation and maintenance of natural processes and then to see that the municipality acquires them, preferably via referendum. Unless the municipality has just recently undertaken such an acquisition, there really should be no argument about making such a move project number one. There are two good reasons for it. The first is obvious: land is neither getting any cheaper, nor is it getting more plentiful. For most municipalities there really is a deadline for this kind of action and that deadline is right around the corner. Soon the high priority land identified by the conservation group will either be gone or carry a price tag that is simply out of sight.

The second reason for making this kind of acquisition referendum the first project is no less important. It has to do with strategy. If the official conservation commission or council wants to get off to a good start, it must build a foundation of awareness of the need for open space preservation within the community. And there is no better way to build it than to force the citizens to come to grips in a referendum. Here is the best of all possible platforms for all that can be said about the constructive role that open space preservation can play in the environmental, social and economic aspects of the community. And, as Chapter III points out, the acquisition placed before the voters should be significant enough to command their attention and to enlist the allegiance of various segments of community leadership. There is every indication that the referendums can succeed. If there are those who fear that one big purchase will destroy the capacity for future acquisitions, they need only be reminded of the insurance salesman's maxim: "The best prospect is the one who owns the most."

Once a referendum has been passed, the conservation commission or council can turn to other methods of preser-

Continuing Programs

vation and they can turn to them with authority, knowledgeability and the backing of the community as well as its elected officials. Large landowners can be sounded out concerning their philanthropic potential for gifts of fee or easement. There are developers to be worked with, particularly in respect to preserving systems of open space by pooling open areas running from one development to the next. The local group can work with private acquisition efforts in cooperative programs, for open space is open space whether it is an Audubon Sanctuary, a town park, or a biology teaching area owned by the public school district. The conservation commission or council can safely and legitimately encourage cash donations for municipal acquisition of sites that may be farther down the priority list but of great interest and importance to various community organizations or groups. There is indeed an incredible array of action opportunities for an official agency to undertake.

What really matters of course is not a slavish adherence to the mechanics of open space preservation or even to governmental organization, but a community's image of itself. Saving open space is no more or less than an expression of community pride—in this case pride in its natural landscape. It is this image that municipal officials and civic leaders must bring into focus. They must force their fellow citizens to see that their heritage is not indestructible, but very much the opposite—a legacy that is as fragile as it is priceless.

Selected Bibliography

Babcock, Richard F., *The Zoning Game* (Madison: The University of Wisconsin Press, 1966). Plain talk about zoning.

Brenneman, Russell L., *Private Approaches to the Preservation of Open Land* (New London, Connecticut: The Conservation and Research Foundation, 1967). A good legal text dealing with donation of fee or easements.

Department of Commerce, *Zoning for Small Towns and Rural Counties* (Washington, D.C.: U. S. Government Printing Office, 1967). Contains interesting approaches for agricultural areas, slopes, flood plains, historical and scenic areas and zoning for new towns.

Daane, Kenneth E., *The Economic Implications of the Regional Park System in Maricopa County* (Tempe, Arizona: Bureau of Business Services, College of Business Administration, Arizona State University, 1964). A good model for this kind of study.

DeBard, Stuart, *The Conservation Commission Handbook* (Massachusetts Association of Conservation Commissions, 84 State Street, Boston, Massachusetts, 1967). This is a remarkable how-to manual dealing with practically every technical matter encountered by a municipality in preserving open space.

Hawkins, Donald E. (Editor) and Tindall, Barry S. (Associate Editor), *Recreation and Park Yearbook* (Washington, D.C.: National Recreation and Park Association, 1967). Information on Federal and State programs as well as helpful statistics for all levels of government.

Norcross, Carl, *Open Space Communities in the Marketplace* (Washington, D.C.: Urban Land Institute, 1966). An extraordinarily good report on actual experience in cluster development. Directed principally at the builder and developer.

Office of Economic Opportunity, *Catalogue of Federal Assistance Programs* (Washington, D.C., 1967). Describes 459 programs.

Open Space Action Institute, *Open Space Preservation Methods* (New York, 1967). This is an edited transcript of a conference dealing with easements, cluster development, land philanthropy and other innovative methods of preservation.

Open Space Action Institute, *Stewardship: The Land, The Landowner, The Metropolis* (New York, 1965). A manual for private landowners in the New York Metropolitan Region dealing with preservation methods.

Regional Plan Association, *Public Participation in Regional Planning* (New York, 1967). Reports on research conducted by RPA among 5,600 informed citizens to determine their ideas on realistic planning choices relating to housing, transportation, open space and other factors.

Regional Plan Association, *The Race for Open Space* (New York, 1960). Still a good source book for open space statistics in the New York region as well as providing sound recommendations for action.

Regional Plan Association, *The Region's Growth* (New York, 1967). Projects growth in the New York region to the year 2000 in terms of population, jobs, households, income.

Regional Plan Association, *Spread City* (New York, 1962). "Projections of development trends and the issues they pose" for the New York metropolitan region.

Rienow, Robert and Rienow, Leona Train, *Moment in the Sun* (New York: The Dial Press, 1967). A kind of "fact book" compiling the ecological horrors of twentieth century population growth and urbanization.

Siegal, Shirley Adelson, *The Law of Open Space* (New York: Regional Plan Association, 1960). A general review of legal aspects in the New York region.

Strong, Ann Louise, *Open Space for Urban America* (for the Department of Housing and Urban Development. Washington, D.C.: U.S. Government Printing Office, 1965). A comprehensive report on open space planning and action at all levels of government.

Wallace, David A., et al, *Metropolitan Open Space from Natural Processes* (Institute for Environmental Studies, University of Pennsylvania, 1967). A valuable academic treatise developing Ian McHarg's "Natural Process" theory in land planning terms.

Whyte, William H., *Cluster Development* (New York: American Conservation Association, 1964). An authoritative report on the functions, forms and economics of cluster planning.

Whyte, William H., *Open Space Action* (Washington, D.C.: Outdoor Recreation Resources Review Commission, U.S. Government Printing Office, 1962). Includes essays on tax abatement, cluster and less than fee rights, voluminous appendix providing various statutes and deed forms.

Whyte, William H., *Securing Open Space for Urban America: Conservation Easements* (Washington, D.C.: Urban Land Institute, 1959). A full discussion of the subject and still the best.

Williams, Norman, Jr. *Land Acquisition for Outdoor Recreation: Analysis of Selected Legal Problems* (Washington, D.C.: Outdoor Recreation Resources Review Commission, U.S. Government Printing Office, 1966). A useful annotated discussion of various forms of acquisition.

Wood, Robert C., *Suburbia: Its People and Their Politics* (Boston: Houghton Mifflin, 1958). For an understanding of how suburbia works—and why—this is the book to read.

100

Appendix

RAMAPO DRAINAGE COMMISSION LEGISLATION

LOCAL LAW REGULATING DRAINAGE, THE USE, OBSTRUC-
TION OR DIVERSION OF STREAMS AND WATER COURSES,
AND THE ESTABLISHMENT OF A DRAINAGE COMMISSION
IN THE TOWN OF RAMAPO, COUNTY OF ROCKLAND, STATE
OF NEW YORK.

Be it enacted by the Town Board of the Town of Ramapo, State of New York, as follows:

The Code of the Town of Ramapo is hereby amended by changing Chapter 14 to read as follows:

Section 14-1   LEGISLATIVE INTENT

A. The rapid growth in the Town of Ramapo and consequent improvement and construction of buildings, paved surfaces, roads, and other improvements has altered in the past and continues to alter the natural flow of surface waters on the land which together with the construction of culverts, drains and ditches for the carrying off of surface waters has both increased the quantity of storm and surface drainage and amplified in quantity and intensity the extent of run-off and surface flow, thus leading to present and potential flooding of property and homes, soil erosion, dangers to health, injury and destruction of property. The development of appropriate facilities to meet the needs of the community has been inadequate with the consequent result that a serious problem and danger has arisen to the health, welfare, well-being and property in the Town of Ramapo.

It is the intention of the Town Board to protect the citizens of the Town of Ramapo, to prevent the dangers arising from improper drainage, improper drainage facilities in areas of poor drainage and high ground water, inadequate construction of drainage facilities, and unwise diversion, use and obstruction of streams and water courses and to plan for the present and future use of drainage systems and water courses through the establishment of a Town Drainage Commission.

B. The provisions of this Law shall be applicable to those portions of the Town of Ramapo outside the limits of any incorporated village.

Section 14-2   PROHIBITED ACTS

A. Except as hereinafter provided it shall be unlawful for any person, firm, entity or corporation to:

(1) place, deposit or permit to be placed or deposited any debris, fill, sand, stone or other solid materials of any kind or nature or construction of any kind into or across any stream, ditch, culvert, pipe, water course or other drainage system shown on the Official Map of the Town of Ramapo;

(2) construct and/or place any ditch, pipe, culvert or artificial water course of any kind or nature which shall collect and direct the flow of natural surface waters or drainage or increase in intensity or quantity the flow of surface waters or drainage from paved surfaces, structures, roads or improvements directly into any stream, ditch, culvert, pipe or water course or other drainage system shown on the Official Map of the Town of Ramapo;

(3) fill, obstruct, dam, divert or otherwise change or alter the natural or artificial flow of waters or drainage or the intensity or quantity of flow, through any stream, ditch, pipe, culvert, water course or other improvement or drainage system shown on the Official Map of the Town of Ramapo.

Section 14-3   CORRECTION OF EXISTING CONDITIONS

A. Except as hereinafter provided, all existing obstructions, dams, diversions, construction of any kind, deposits of debris, fill, sand, stone or other solid materials or other alterations or diversions of the natural flow of water or the intensity or quantity of flow, through, across or to any stream, ditch, culvert, water course or other drainage system shown on the Official Map of the Town of Ramapo which:

(1) causes the inundation of real property and/or buildings on other premises, or

(2) in the determination of the Drainage Commission constitutes an undue burden upon the official drainage system or hampers the proper present or future course of development of the official drainage system, or

(3) in the determination of the Drainage Commission, presently constitutes or in the reasonably foreseeable future will constitute a danger or hazard to the well-being, safety or general welfare of the residents of the Town or any property located therein;

shall be removed or corrected by the owners of the premises upon which said obstructions, dams, diversions, construction, deposits or other alterations of the natural flow of water are situated, within sixty (60) days after written notice to remove or correct same from the Town Board.

Section 14-4   PERMITTED ACTS

A. The prohibited acts and correction of existing conditions set forth in Sections 14-2 and 14-3 hereof shall have no application to work done pursuant to the authority of an agency of the Town of Ramapo, County of Rockland, State of New York and United States of America.

B. The acts set forth in Section 14-2 hereof are permissible if done pursuant to the terms and conditions of a permit obtained from the Town Clerk of the Town of Ramapo, or pursuant to an approved and filed subdivision map or a building permit or special permit carrying site development plan approval by the Planning Board.

Section 14-5   PROCEDURE FOR OBTAINING A PERMIT

A. All applicants for a permit to do any of the acts prohibited by Section 14-2 or to fill, divert, dam or in any way alter the natural flow of a stream, ditch, culvert, water course, or other drainage system shown on the Official Map of the Town of Ramapo, except any applicant filing a proposed subdivision with the Planning Board, shall present plans and specifications prepared by a licensed professional engineer for the proposed change to the Town Clerk who shall thereupon cause the said plans and specifications to be examined by the Town Engineer or such consulting engineer as shall be designated by the Drainage Commission. Whenever the cost of the proposed improvement does not exceed the sum of $100.00, the plans and specifications do not have to be prepared by a licensed professional engineer. After the Town Engineer or consulting engineer shall have reviewed the proposed plans and specifications, the Town Engineer or consulting engineer shall forward a report and recommendation to the Drainage Commission of the Town of Ramapo. Wherever an application for a permit to do an act set forth above affects land lying partly within and partly without lands requiring subdivision approval or site development plan approval, an application for a permit for that part of the premises lying outside of the subdivision or outside of the land requiring site plan approval shall be submitted to the Town Clerk and forwarded by the Engineer to the Drainage Commission.

B. The Drainage Commission shall review the report and recommendations of the Town Engineer or consulting engineer together with the proposed plans and specifications and shall render its determination to the Town Clerk within forty-five (45) days. If the Drainage Commission shall approve the proposed changes, the Town Clerk shall issue a permit therefor.

C. Wherever the approval of the Drainage Commission shall, in the opinion of the Drainage Commission, affect or require a change or addition to the Official Map, the Town Clerk shall, prior to the issuance of any permit, place the matter on the agenda of the Town Board for a public hearing. At least ten (10) days notice of a public hearing on the proposed action with reference to the change in the official map shall be published in the official newspaper of the Town. Prior to making any such addition or change, the Town Board shall refer the matter to the Planning Board for report thereon, which report shall be returned by the Planning Board within thirty (30) days of such reference. The addition and change, when adopted, shall become a part of the official map of the Town of Ramapo and shall be deemed to be final and conclusive with respect to the location of the drainage systems shown thereon.

D. Prior to the issuance of the permit above, each applicant shall pay to the Town Clerk a fee of 2 per cent of the estimated cost of improvements or construction, as determined by the Town Engineer or consulting engineer, representing the actual cost to the Town for review and inspection of the applicant's plans and specifications.

E. The Town Engineer may, in his discretion, refer any problems concerning drainage to the Drainage Commission for their review and recommendations and shall refer such matters to the Drainage Commission in any case where the matter will require a change in the Official Map of the Town of Ramapo.

Section 14-6 CREATION AND ORGANIZATION OF THE DRAINAGE COMMISSION

A. The Town Board is hereby authorized and empowered to create a Drainage Commission which shall consist of five members, who shall be especially qualified by reason of training or experience in engineering, community planning or other relevant business or profession. The members of the Drainage Commission shall be appointed by the Town Board and the Town Board shall designate a chairman from the members. The Town Board may provide for compensation to be paid to said members and a secretary and provide for such other expenses as may be necessary and proper, including the services of a consulting engineer upon the recommendation of the Drainage Commission, not exceeding in all the appropriations that may be made by the Town Board for such Drainage Commission. The Town Board is hereby authorized to make such appropriation as it may see fit for such expenses. Of the members first appointed, one shall hold office for the term of one year, one for the term of two years, one for the term of three years, one for the term of four years and one for the term of five years from and after his or her appointment. Their successors shall be appointed for a term of five years from and after the expiration of the terms of their predecessors in office. If a vacancy shall occur otherwise than by expiration of a term it shall be filled by the Town Board by appointment for the unexpired term. The Drainage Commission shall hold a minimum of ten (10) meetings per year and at least monthly whenever any application for permit, request from any agency of the Town or other subject is pending before the Commission. Meetings of the Drainage Commission shall be held at such times as the Commission may determine and at such other times at the call of the chairman or direction of the Town Board. Three members of such Commission shall constitute a quorum for the transaction of business. The Commission shall keep minutes of its proceedings showing the vote of each member upon any question or, if absent or failing to vote, indicating such fact, and shall also keep records of its official actions.

B. Every decision, recommendation or determination of the Commission shall be filed within ten (10) days in the office of the Town Clerk and shall be a public record. The Drainage Commission shall have the power to adopt, amend and repeal rules and regulations governing its procedure and transaction of business after a public hearing held at least ten (10) days after publication of a notice setting forth the proposed rules and regulations in the official Town newspaper. All rules and regulations shall be approved by the Town Board prior to coming into effect. Such rules and regulations and any amendments or repeal thereof shall take effect immediately upon filing in the office of the Town Clerk, after such approval of the Town Board.

C. The Town Engineer or consulting engineer shall furnish to the Drainage Commission such recommendations and engineering data as the Commission shall request and require and the Town Engineer or consulting engineer shall advise the Commission on all other matters within the powers and duties of the Commission and upon request shall be present at the meetings and deliberations of the Commission.

Section 14-7 DUTIES AND POWERS OF THE DRAINAGE COMMISSION

A. The Drainage Commission shall investigate and recommend action to the Town Board regarding violations of the provisions of this local law.

B. The Drainage Commission shall investigate and report upon drainage problems referred to it by the Town Board, Town officials, or any Commission or agency of the Town.

C. The Drainage Commission shall have the power to review and recommend to the Town Board all proposed changes to the Official Map of the Town of Ramapo, concerning drainage systems, except those shown upon subdivision plats or site plan approvals passed upon by the Planning Board.

D. Upon request of the Planning Board the Drainage Commission shall have the power to review and make recommendations to the Planning Board concerning any of the following:

(1) Drainage and ground water conditions lying within a subdivision or any premises for which site-plan approval is required of the Planning Board and proper requirements for treating such conditions if feasible;

(2) Proper requirements for all off-site easements, construction, servitudes, ditches, culverts, pipes, water courses and drainage systems not lying within a

proposed subdivision or premises for which site-plan approval is required, in order to properly conduct surface water and run-off and ground water from a proposed subdivision or premises for which site-plan approval is required to a stream, ditch, culvert, water course or other drainage system shown on the Official Map of the Town of Ramapo.

E. The Drainage Commission shall cause studies to be made of matters concerning drainage and shall recommend and propose to the Town Board legislation concerning drainage, involving ordinances, local laws, or amendments to the subdivision regulations.

F. The Drainage Commission shall coordinate Town Drainage programs with drainage programs of villages and municipalities within the Town and with adjacent municipalities and Towns and the County of Rockland.

Section 14-8   PENALTIES AND CORRECTIVE ACTION

A. Any person, firm, entity or corporation found to be violating any provisions of this local law, shall be served with a written notice at the direction of the Town Board stating the nature of the violation and providing a 60-day time limit for the satisfactory correction thereof. The offender shall, within the period stated in such notice, correct or remove all violations.

B. Any persons, firm, entity or corporation who shall continue any violation beyond the time limit provided for in subdivision "A" above shall be guilty of a misdemeanor, and upon conviction thereof be fined in an amount not exceeding $200.00 for each violation. Each week in which such violation shall continue shall be deemed a separate offense.

C. In the event that any person, firm, entity or corporation shall continue any violation beyond the time limit provided for in subdivision "A" above the Town Board may direct the Town Attorney to apply to the Supreme Court in the Ninth Judicial District for an order directing that the violation be corrected or removed, and that all costs and expenses incurred by the Town of Ramapo in connection with the proceedings, including the actual cost of correction or removal, shall be assessed against the offenders.

D. Any person, firm, entity or corporation violating any of the provisions of this local law shall become liable to the Town for any expense or loss or damage occasioned the Town by reason of such violation.

Section 14-9   VALIDITY

A. All ordinances and local laws or parts of ordinances and local laws in conflict herewith are hereby repealed.

B. The invalidity of any word, Section, clause, sentence, section, part or provision of this local law shall not affect the validity of any other part of this local law which can be given effect without such invalid part or parts.

C. It is not intended by this local law to repeal by implication any existing or future rules or regulations of the Rockland County Drainage Commission, it being intended that such rules or regulations shall supercede the within local law.

D. Chapter 14 of the Code of the Town of Ramapo (The General Ordinances of the Town), entitled Filling or Diversion of Streams and Water Courses, adopted by the Town Board of the Town of Ramapo, February 26, 1962, is hereby repealed.

Section 14-10

This local law shall take effect immediately.

RAMAPO INTERIM
DEVELOPMENT LAW

LOCAL LAW REGULATING FOR AN INTERIM PERIOD THE
ISSUANCE OF BUILDING PERMITS AND THE APPROVAL
OF SUBDIVISION PLATS IN AREAS OF THE TOWN AFFECT-
ED BY PROSPECTIVE AMENDMENTS TO THE ZONING
ORDINANCE OF THE TOWN OF RAMAPO PURSUANT TO
THE PROPOSED TOWN MASTER PLAN PREPARED BY THE
TOWN PLANNING BOARD AS NOTICED FOR PUBLIC HEAR-
ING AND ADOPTION AND CONCERNING FUTURE PROSPEC-
TIVE AMENDMENTS TO THE TOWN ZONING ORDINANCE.

Be it enacted by the Town Board of the Town of Ramapo, State of New
York, as follows:

The Code of the Town of Ramapo is hereby amended by adding Chapter
19 to read as follows:

Section 19-1 TITLE

This local law shall be known and may be cited as the "Interim Development Law of the Town of Ramapo".

Section 19-2 LEGISLATIVE INTENT AND FINDINGS OF FACT

A. *Background.*

The Town of Ramapo in Rockland County, New York, being a suburb of
the New York-New Jersey metropolitan region, with its center in New York
City, approximately thirty miles from the center of the Town of Ramapo, has
been experiencing unprecedented and rapid growth with respect to population, housing, economy, land development and utilization of resources for the
past decade. Schools, roads, public services and facilities have been and are
being constructed to meet the needs of the Town's growing population but
these services and facilities have been unable to keep pace with the ever
growing public need. Faced with a number of major physical, social and fiscal
problems caused by this rapid and unprecedented growth in relation to drainage, road construction, sewage disposal, school and library needs and other new
or expanded needs for public services and concerned with the overall quality,
density and character of land development within the community, the Town
of Ramapo has undertaken a comprehensive program to prepare a master plan
to guide its future development which program was conceived during 1963 and
officially started in February, 1964, under the Urban Planning Assistance Program of the Housing Act of 1954, as amended, with the assistance of Federal
and State funds.

The comprehensive planning program is being accomplished by the Town
Planning Board with the Rockland County Planning Board staff serving in the
capacity of planning consultants to the Town Planning Board with close liaison
maintained with the Town Board and all Town agencies and officials.

The planning program has included a study and analysis of the Town's
physical resources, population trends and characteristics, economic and business activity, existing land use and zoning, community facilities, roads and
transportation facilities, and fiscal trends and available financial resources.

As a result of this study a comprehensive master plan, pursuant to Section 272-a of the Town Law of the State of New York, said plan commonly being referred to as the Town of Ramapo Development Plan, embodying all of the purposes of the said statute, has been prepared incorporating recommendations for the proposed future residential, commercial, industrial and public land uses, community facilities including future schools, recreation and other public facilities, road and highway improvements. In addition the comprehensive planning program includes the preparation of: (a) specific recommendations for the revision and amendment of the Town of Ramapo Zoning Ordinance in accordance with the comprehensive master plan; (b) specific recommendations for revision of the Town Subdivision Regulations; (c) specific recommendations for the establishment of a Town Official Map; and (d) a capital improvement program including recommendations of priorities; and (e) recommendations for appropriate planning standards with regard to street improvements and community facilities.

B. *Legislative Findings of Fact.*

The Town Board does hereby find that pending the necessary preliminaries and hearings incident to proper decisions upon the adoption and the terms of the revision and amendments of the Town of Ramapo Zoning Ordinance, in accordance with the comprehensive master plan set forth above, that unless reasonable measures are taken for a reasonable interim period to protect the public interest by preserving the integrity of said plan until the appropriate amendments to the Zoning Ordinance are adopted and become effective, any significant variations in the areas where the master plan recommends changes in the existing zoning ordinance will destroy the integrity of the master plan and its basic purposes and comprehensive aspects.

C. *Legislative Intent.*

It is the intention of the Town Board to protect the comprehensive master plan and to insure its implementation by hereby adopting, pursuant to the authority vested in the Town Board, reasonable interim legislation for a reasonable time during consideration of the aforesaid proposed zoning changes, to protect the public interest and welfare and prevent a race of diligence between propery owners and the Town during consideration of zone changes, which would in many instances result in the establishment of a pattern of land use and development which would be inconsistent with the master plan and violate its basic intent and purpose and fail to protect the community and its general welfare.

It is the purpose and scope of this law to define areas of the Town which are affected by proposed amendments to the zoning ordinance which would result from the implementation of recommendations of the master plan. The Town Board has included only those significant areas which have been recommended by the Town of Ramapo Planning Board as essential to preservation of the master plan and in the best interests of the community and its health, safety, morals and general welfare, and has further provided for a review and appeals procedure to avoid any inequities and undue hardships in the application of this law.

D. *The provisions of this Law shall be applicable to those portions of, the Town of Ramapo outside the limits of any incorporated village.*

109

(B)

Section 19-3 ESTABLISHMENT OF AREAS AFFECTED BY PROPOSED MASTER PLAN, PROPOSED AMENDMENTS TO ZONING ORDINANCE PURSUANT TO SAID PLAN

The Town of Ramapo is hereby divided into the following areas, the respective color for each type of area being set forth opposite its title, which areas and boundaries of such areas are designated on copies of the Official Zoning Map of the Town of Ramapo, referred to in Section 19-4 as the Interim Development Map with their respective colors.

Title	Color
(a) Residential Area to be changed to residential area with greater plot size	Blue
(b) Residential Area to be changed to non-residential area	Blue
(c) Non-Residential Area or mixed non-residential-residential area to be changed to residential area	Blue
(d) Non-residential or mixed non-residential-residential area to be changed to other non-residential area	Blue
(e) All other areas	White or Uncolored

Each such area shall be designated on the Interim Development Map referred to in Section 19-4 and elsewhere in the text of this law by its color only.

Section 19-4 MAP OF AREAS AFFECTED BY PROPOSED MASTER PLAN AND AMENDMENTS TO ZONING ORDINANCE PURSUANT THERETO

The areas and boundaries of such areas referred to in Section 19-3 are hereby established (a) as shown on the map entitled "Zoning Map of the Town of Ramapo, February, 1965 edition" and (b) as specified in Section 19-5. Such map, referred to herein as the "Interim Development Map" together with everything shown thereon, including the colors of the areas referred to in Section 19-3, is hereby made a part of this local law to be so certified by the Town Clerk.

Section 19-5 AREA BOUNDARIES ON INTERIM DEVELOPMENT MAP

Area boundaries encompassing the areas referred to in Section 19-3, shown on the Interim Development Map, shall follow streets, New York State Thruway, any parkway, interstate or municipal park boundaries, public utility rights-of-way, streams, railroads or zoning district lines, as defined in Chapter 46, Section 46-7 of the Code of the Town of Ramapo.

Section 19-6 SCOPE OF CONTROLS

A. During the period of ninety (90) days following the effective date of this local law:

1. No building or structure shall be constructed or erected, nor shall any building permit be issued by the Building Inspector of the Town of Ramapo for the construction or erection of any such building or structure on any lot or lots or property lying within any area marked in blue upon the Interim Development Map.

2. The Planning Board of the Town of Ramapo shall not grant any preliminary approval to a subdivision plat, regardless of the fact that such subdivision plat has been submitted to the Planning Board prior to the effective date of this law, for any subdivision plat which lies wholly or partially within the areas marked in blue as shown upon the Interim Development Map.

B. Nothing contained in this law shall be deemed to affect in any way whatsoever the granting, issuance and/or approval of building permits, site-plan approval and/or subdivision approval, for lots, buildings, structures, property and/or subdivision plats lying wholly within a white area on the Interim Development Map, nor shall building permits be denied to any subdivision in any area shown on the Interim Development Map which has received final approval from the Planning Board.

C. (1) The Town Board reserves the power to direct the Building Inspector to revoke or rescind any building permits issued in contravention to the provisions of this local law on or after the date of publication of the legal notice establishing the public hearing pertaining to adoption of this law.

(2) Any building permit granted prior to the date of publication of the notice of public hearing as set forth above shall remain valid and inviolate and shall not in any way be affected or rescinded by the operation of this law.

Section 19-7 APPEAL PROVISIONS

A. The Town Board shall have the power to vary or modify the application of any provision of this local law upon its determination in its absolute legislative discretion, that such variance or modification is consistent with the spirit of the comprehensive master plan upon which this local law is based and with the health, safety, morals and general welfare of the Town.

B. Upon receiving any application for such variance or modification, the Town Board shall refer such application to the Planning Board of the Town of Ramapo for a report of said Planning Board with respect to the effect of the prospective variance or modification upon the said master plan. The Supervisor, to expedite appeal, shall forward all applications for relief within twenty-four hours after receipt of same in his office to the Town Planning Board for its report. Such report shall be returned by the Planning Board to the Town Board within fifteen days of such reference and shall be placed upon the next agenda of the Town Board.

Section 19-8 PENALTIES

Any person, firm, entity or corporation who shall construct, erect, enlarge or alter structurally, any building or structure, in violation of the provisions of this local law or shall otherwise violate any of the provisions of this local law shall be subject to the penalties set forth in Chapter 46, Section 46-29 of the Code of the Town of Ramapo.

Section 19-9 VALIDITY

The invalidity of any word, section, clause, paragraph, sentence, part of provision of this local law shall not effect the validity of any other part of this local law which can be given effect without such invalid part or parts.

Section 19-10 EFFECTIVE DATE

This local law shall take effect immediately.

(C)

RAMAPO AVERAGE DENSITY LAW

FOR THE IMPLEMENTATION OF SECTION 281
OF THE TOWN LAW OF THE STATE OF NEW YORK

WHEREAS, the Town Board is empowered to authorize the Planning Board, simultaneously with the approval of a plat, to modify applicable provisions of the Zoning Ordinance of the Town of Ramapo, all pursuant to the provisions of Section 281 of the Town Law of the State of New York, and

WHEREAS, the purpose of such authorization is to enable and encourage flexibility of design and development of land in such manner as to promote the most appropriate use of land, to facilitate the adequate and economic use of streets and utilities and to preserve the natural and scenic qualities of open lands, and

WHEREAS, the Town Board has determined to empower the Planning Board to mandate the use of Density Zoning for a subdivision plat whether or not the applicant has consented to the use of Density Zoning,

NOW, THEREFORE, BE IT RESOLVED that the following shall be the procedure for the implementation of the aforesaid Section 281 of the Town Law of the State of New York:

(1) After the submission of the pre-preliminary plat to the Planning Board of the Town of Ramapo, if either the applicant requests the use of density zoning or the Planning Board on its own motion determines that density zoning is suitable for the plat, then the pre-preliminary plat, together with a Planning Board study setting forth the basis for recommending utilization of the procedures in Section 281, shall be submitted to the Town Board.

(2) Upon submission of the pre-preliminary plat and recommendations, the Town Board shall expeditiously cause to be published in the official newspaper of the Town, a notice stating that an application for the utilization of the provisions of Section 281 of the Town Law has been submitted to the Town Board and shall generally describe the area covered in the application, and that such application will be placed on the agenda of the Town Board meeting, which meeting date shall be no less than ten nor more than twenty days subsequent to the date of publication of the aforesaid notice. The pur-Town Board in determining whether or not to authorize the Planning Board, by resolution, to modify the provisions of the Zoning Ordinance, all as is set forth in Section 281 of the Town Law.

(3) Such discussion shall be held to further assist the Town Board in setting forth the conditions to be incorporated in such resolution, if the Town Board determines that the Planning Board shall be so authorized to modify the applicable provisions of the Zoning Ordinance.

(4) In the event that the plat shows lands available for a sewer plant or school purposes, the Town Board will conduct a public hearing on the matter in lieu of placing the matter on the agenda, as set forth in subdivision (2) hereof. Such public hearing shall be held after due notice in the official newspaper of the Town, such notice to be published not less than ten nor more than twenty days prior to such public hearing.

(5) If the Town Board determines that the pre-preliminary plat is suitable for utilization of the procedures allowed under Section 281, the Town Board shall adopt a resolution containing the conditions required by Section 281,

namely, that the procedures shall be applicable only to lands zoned for residential purposes and its application shall result in a permitted number of dwelling units which shall in no case exceed the number which could be permitted, in the Planning Board's judgment, if the land were subdivided into lots conforming to the minimum lot size and density requirements of the Zoning Ordinance applicable to the district or districts in which such land is situated and conforming to all other applicable requirements. Whether or not the Planning Board initiates the request for use of Section 281, if the Town Board adopts a resolution granting the Planning Board the use of Section 281, the Planning Board shall have the option of requiring the use of Section 281 for this parcel unless the application for subdivision is withdrawn.

(6) Another condition required by Section 281 is that if the application of this procedure results in a plat showing land available for park, recreation, open space or other municipal purposes, directly related to the plat, then conditions as to ownership, use and maintenance of such lands as are necessary to assure the preservation of such lands for their intended purposes shall be set forth.

Other conditions to be included by the Town Board shall include permission for the Planning Board to reduce area, plot width, yard requirements, frontage, etc. in keeping with good planning practice. In no event shall the minimum plot area of any plot in an RR-80, RR-50, R-40, R-35 or R-25 zoning district be reduced below 15,000 square feet nor shall minimum plot width be reduced to less than 90 feet. In an R-15 Zoning District the minimum plot area shall be 12,000 square feet and the minimum plot width 75 feet. The land reserved by the Planning Board need not be all contiguous but may consist of one large parcel or strips of land lying between lots shown on the subdivision plat or any other design or location as in the Planning Board's judgment shall encourage the most appropriate use of the land.

(7) Before the Town Board shall determine that such pre-preliminary plat is suitable for the procedures under Section 281, it shall find that the above standards and conditions will generally be met, that the appropriate use of adjoining land is safeguarded, that the proposed plan is consistent with the general welfare, that the proposed use, if any, of open land will tend to enhance the natural features and aesthetics of the land and roads, that the proposed changes in the applicable zoning regulations are reasonable and that the public health, safety and welfare will be protected.

(8) In the event the procedures of Section 281 of the Town Law are utilized in an R-15 district, the lands available for municipal use shall be utilized solely for park, open area or drainage purposes.

(9) The Town Board shall not consider any land available for park, recreation, open space or other municipal. purposes, unless such land shall have a minimum of two acres.

(10) Upon determination by the Town Board that such pre-preliminary plat is suitable for the procedures under Section 281 and subsequent to the resolution authorizing the Planning Board to proceed, a preliminary plat meeting all of the requirements of the resolution shall be presented to the Planning Board of the Town of Ramapo and thereafter the Planning Board of the Town of Ramapo shall proceed with the required public hearings and all other requirements as set forth by statute.

(C)

(11) Should the Town Board consider amending or rescinding this resolution, or any part thereof, a public hearing shall be duly held by the Town Board no more than twenty nor less than ten days after publication of such notice in the official newspaper of the Town, before the Town Board takes any action in amending or rescinding this resolution, or any part thereof.

(12) The invalidity of any word, section, clause, sentence, part or provision of this resolution, shall not affect the validity of any other part of this resolution which can be given effect without such invalid part or parts.

July 31, 1967

RAMAPO DEVELOPMENT EASEMENT ACQUISITION LAW (D)

Local Law Establishing a DEVELOPMENT EASEMENT ACQUI-
SITION COMMISSION IN THE TOWN OF RAMAPO, COUNTY
OF ROCKLAND, STATE OF NEW YORK, for the Purpose of Main-
taining Lands as Open Space and Areas, Controlling the Rate of
Development of the Town and Enhancing the Conservation of Natural
and Scenic Resources.

§11-1. Title.
§11-2. Legislative Intent, Findings of Fact and Scope of Controls.
§11-3. Creation and Organization of the Development Easement Acquisition
     Commission.
§11-4. Duties and Powers of the Development Easement Acquisition Commis-
     sion.
§11-5. Validity.
§11-6 Effective Date.

Be it enacted by the Town Board of the Town of Ramapo as follows:

§11-1. Title

This local law shall be known and may be cited as the "Development Easement Acquisition Law of the Town of Ramapo".

§11-2. Legislative Intent and Findings of Fact

A. *Legislative Intent*

The Town of Ramapo, being a suburb of the New York-New Jersey metropolitan region, has been experiencing unprecedented and rapid growth with
respect to population, housing, economy, land development and utilization of
resources. Schools, roads, sewers, drainage facilities, parks, public services and
facilities have been and are being constructed to meet the needs of the burgeoning population but these services and facilities have been unable to be
provided so as to keep pace with the ever growing public need, resulting in
serious diminishment of the present and potential value of the Town's development.

The rapid growth and spread of urban development is creating encroachment upon and elimination of the open areas and spaces of the Town, including many having significant scenic or aesthetic values, which areas and spaces
if preserved and maintained in their present open state would constitute important physical, social, aesthetic and economic assets to existing or impending Town development and would enhance the present or potential value of
the Town's development.

Faced with these problems the Town of Ramapo undertook, completed and
adopted a Master Plan pursuant to Section 272-a of the Town Law of the
State of New York, on July 26, 1966, which Master Plan incorporates recommendations for preserving open space and areas, creation of public parks and
facilities, protection of drainage basins, streams and natural land, wood and
field resources.

The Town of Ramapo has adopted a comprehensive amendment to the
zoning ordinance, is preparing subdivision regulations, an official map, a capital
budget, interim development law and other laws and regulations to control and
limit the density and regulate the rate of growth of the Town so as to provide 115

(D)

services and facilities to keep pace with the needs of the community and to protect and preserve the open spaces and areas of the Town for the purpose of the Master Plan set for the above, whose loss would be permanent and irreparable. The Town of Ramapo has therefore determined to utilize development easements and grants to remove large open areas of the Town from immediate development so as to enhance the present or potential value of the Town's development by bringing needed services and facilities to existing and potential development and to provide the amenities and permanent value of open space to the people of the community.

The Town Board intends that the program be a voluntary one on the part of the land owner. Numerous holders of large tracts of land and open space in the Town, who do not have plans for developing the property, are unable to continue to hold the property in a farming, agricultural, natural or recreational state without serious economic deprivation due to rising real property taxation. There will now be a legal basis for providing tax relief for agricultural, natural, recreational or aesthetic use of land, valuable to the community in its open state which will at the same time achieve the purposes of controlled growth to enhance the value of the Town's development for the period of the development easements and rights obtained and further the need of the community for open space. Properties not accepted within the development easement program will be assessed at the full market value of the property for purposes of real property taxation.

The Town Board intends to utilize herein the full powers granted to it pursuant to Section 247 of the General Municipal Law as well as all other powers granted and reserved to the Town in the Municipal Home Rule Law, Statute of Local Governments, Town Law and Constitution of the State of New York.

B. *Legislative Findings of Fact*

The Town Board does hereby find that it is necessary for the controlled, sound and proper town development, and in the public interest of the people of the Town of Ramapo for the Town to accept by easement primarily and by gift, grant, bequest, demise, purchase, lease, or otherwise, the acquisition of development easements, rights and interests in land in order to achieve open spaces and areas of natural and scenic beauty, to maintain and enhance the conservation of natural and scenic resources and to enhance the value of the Town's development by controlling the rate of growth of development of the community within the ability of the Town to furnish needed services and facilities to its people.

§11-3. Creation and Organization of the Development Easement Acquisition Commission

A. The Town Board is hereby authorized and empowered to create a Development Easement Acquisition Commission which shall consist of seven (7) members, none of whom shall hold any other elective or appointive office in the Government of the Town of Ramapo. The initial appointments to the Commission shall be for terms of one, two, three, four, five, six and seven years, respectively. Successors to the Commission shall be appointed for a term of seven (7) years following the expiration of the terms of their predecessors in office. If a vacancy occurs otherwise than by expiration of a term shall be filled by the Town Board for the balance of the unexpired term, by appointment. The Supervisor, the Town Attorney, the Town Assessor and the Chairmen of the Planning Board, Drainage Commission and Recreation Commission, shall serve as Consultants to the Commission and shall receive all notices of commission meetings and be entitled to non-voting participation in Commission meetings. The Town Board shall annually designate the Chairman of the Commission but upon its failure to do so within thirty (30) days of the date of creation of the Commission or on said date in each succeeding year the Commission may proceed to elect a chairman from the membership for the balance of that year. The Town Board may provide for compensation to be paid to the members of the Commission and provide for such other expenses as may be necessary and proper, including the services of any secretaries or technical consultants upon recommendation of the Commission, not exceeding in all the appropriations that may be made by the Town Board for such Commission. The Town Board is hereby authorized to make such appropriation as it may see fit for such expenses. Meetings of the Commission shall be held at such times as the Commission may determine and at such other times at the call of the Supervisor. Four members of the Commission shall constitute a quorum. The Commission shall keep records of its official actions.

B. Every decision, recommendation or determination of the Commission shall be filed within ten (10) days in the Office of the Town Clerk and shall be a public record. The Commission shall have the power to adopt, amend and repeal rules and regulations governing its transaction and business after a public hearing held at least ten (10) days after publication of a notice setting forth the proposed rules and regulations in the official town newspaper.

The rules and regulations shall not be limited to acquisition procedures but may make provision for ameliorative features in the easement documents or otherwise for the prevention of hardship to persons or the heirs of persons who have given development easements so that the purposes of the commission shall be achieved through the encouragement of easement donation and the interests of both the individual and the community be adequately protected. All rules and regulations shall be approved by the Town Board prior to coming into effect. Such rules and regulations and any amendments or repeals thereof shall take effect immediately upon filing in the office of the Town Clerk after such approval by the Town Board.

§11-4. Duties and Powers of the Development Easement Acquisition Commission

A. The Commission shall investigate on its own initiative or upon request of owners of land into the ownership, nature and extent of existing open space or open areas in the Town of Ramapo characterized by natural scenic beauty or whose existing openness, natural condition or present state of use would enhance the present or potential value of abutting or surrounding development, or would maintain or enhance the conservation of natural or scenic resources and which land by remaining in its existing state would further controlled growth and development of the Town.

B. In reaching a determination by the Commission that a parcel of land is suitable for acquisition of development rights by the Town, the Commission shall seek a recommendation where appropriate from any or all of the following: The Recreation Commission, Drainage Commission, Town Planning Board, County Planning Board or any other agency or official of the Town or other municipal corporation as the Commission in its discretion shall determine. The

(D)

Commission shall request the Town Assessor to advise the extent to which acquisition of a development easement, right or other interest shall effect the assessed valuation placed on such open space or area for purposes of real estate taxation by reason of the prospective limitation on future use of the land.

C. The Commission, if it reaches the determination that acquisition of a development easement, right or other interest in a parcel of land would be beneficial to the Town shall communicate with the owner of the land and all encumbrances, mortgages, lienors and holders of interests in the land for the acquisition of interests or rights in the real property by gift, grant, bequest, demise, lease or otherwise constituting a lesser interest than the fee, development easement, right, covenant or other contractual right necessary to achieve the purposes of this law. No development, easement interest or right shall be for a period of less than five (5) years. Where the Commission deems acquisition of the entire fee or any lesser interest in the land essential, and such fee or lesser interest cannot be acquired by gift, grant, bequest or demise or for nominal consideration, a special report shall be furnished to the Town Board concerning the consideration required to obtain such interest.

D. Upon completion of the arrangements for acquisition of the development easement, right or other interests, the legal documents for acquisition of such rights, shall be drawn upon the advice of the Town Attorney and submitted by the Commission to the Town Board; together with the report of the Commission for further action. The Town Board prior to acceptance of any gift, grant, bequest, demise, easement, right or acquisition shall duly advertise same for a public hearing after due notice, posting and publication in the official newspaper of the Town. Upon the Town Board accepting such acquisition, it shall be duly published and posted and the acquisition shall become final and shall be duly recorded ten (10) days thereafter, or after said resolution becomes final under the applicable provisions of Article Seven of the Town Law. After acquisition of any such interest pursuant to this law, the valuation placed on such open space or area for purposes of real estate taxation shall take into account the depreciation fixed by the Town Assessor pursuant to §11-4 (B).

§11-5. Validity

The invalidity of any word, section, clause, sentence, part or provision of this local law shall not affect the validity of any other part of this local law which can be given effect without such invalid part or parts.

§11-6. Effective Date

This local law shall take effect immediately.

Adopted: June 26, 1967

§247. Acquisition of open spaces and areas

1. *Definitions.* For the purposes of this chapter an "open space" or "open area" is any space or area characterized by (1) natural scenic beauty or (2) whose existing openness, natural condition, or present state of use, if retained, would enhance the present or potential value of abutting or surrounding urban development, or would maintain or enhance the conservation of natural or scenic resources.

2. The acquisition of interests or rights in real property for the preservation of open spaces and areas shall constitute a public purpose for which public funds may be expended or advanced, and any county, city, town or village after due notice and a public hearing may acquire, by purchase, gift, grant, bequest, devise, lease or otherwise, the fee or any lesser interest, development right, easement, covenant, or other contractual right necessary to achieve the purposes of this chapter, to land within such municipality. In the case of a village the cost of such acquisition of interests or rights may be incurred wholly at the expense of the village, at the expense of the owners of the lands benefited thereby, or partly at the expense of such owners and partly at the expense of the village at large as a local improvement in the manner provided by article eleven-A of the village law.

3. After acquisition of any such interest pursuant to this act the *valuation placed on such an open space or area for purposes of real estate taxation shall take into account and be limited by the limitation on future use of the land.* Added L.1960, c. 945, §2; amended L.1963, c. 736, eff. April 23, 1963.

§247 — GENERAL MUNICIPAL LAW — Art. 13

Historical Note

Subd. 2 amended by L.1963, c. 736, eff. April 23, 1963, which added last sentence.

Legislative Intent. Laws 1960, c. 945, §1, eff. April 28, 1960, provided:

"It is the intent of the legislature in enacting this chapter to provide a means whereby any county, city, town or village may acquire, by purchase, gift, grant, bequest, devise, lease or otherwise, and through the expenditure of public funds, the fee or any lesser interest or right in real property in order to preserve, through limitation of their future use, open spaces and areas for public use and enjoyment.

"The legislature finds that the rapid growth and spread of urban development is encroaching upon, or eliminating, many open areas and spaces of varied size and character, including many having significant scenic or esthetic values, which areas and spaces if preserved and maintained in their present open state would constitute important physical, social, esthetic or economic assets to existing or impending urban and metropolitan development.

"The legislature hereby declares that it is necessary for sound and proper urban and metropolitan development, and in the public interest of the people of this state for any county, city, town or village to expend or advance public funds for, or to accept by, purchase, gift, grant, bequest, devise, lease or otherwise, the fee or any lesser interest or right in real property to acquire, maintain, improve, protect, limit the future use of or otherwise conserve open spaces and areas within their respective jurisdictions."

119

(F)

HILLSBOROUGH, NEW JERSEY, CLUSTERING ORDINANCE, ARTICLE VIII

ARTICLE VIII

DESIGN STANDARDS

The subdivider shall observe the following requirements and principles of land subdivision in the design of each subdivision or portion thereof.

1. *General*

The subdivision plat shall conform to design standards that will encourage good development patterns within the township. Where either or both an official map or master plan has or have been adopted, the subdivision shall conform to the proposals and conditions shown thereon except that the applicant shall be permitted to propose changes in the master plan requirements at the time of submission of the Sketch Plat. The streets, drainage rights-of-way, school sites, public parks and playgrounds shown on an officially adopted master plan or official map shall be considered in approval of subdivision plats. Where no master plan or official map exists, streets and drainage rights-of-way shall be shown on the final plat in accordance with section 20 of Chapter 433 of the Laws of 1953, and shall be such as to lend themselves to the harmonious development of the township and enhance the public welfare in accordance with the following design standards:

2. *Streets*

(a) The arrangement of streets not shown on the master plan or official map, shall be such as to provide for the appropriate extension of existing streets.

(b) The right-of-way width shall be measured from lot line to lot line and shall conform with the standard specifications governing the construction of roads and streets adopted by the Township Committee of the Township of Hillsborough March, 1948 and the supplements and amendments thereto.

(c) No subdivision showing reserve strips controlling access to streets shall be approved except where the control and disposal of land comprising such strips has been placed in the Township Committee under conditions approved by the Planning Board.

(d) Subdivisions that adjoin or include existing streets that do not conform to widths as shown on the master plan or official map, should either or both be adopted, or the street width requirements described in paragraph 2 (b) of this Article, shall dedicate additional width along either one or both sides of said road. If the subdivision is along one side only, one-half of the required extra width shall be dedicated.

(e) Street intersections shall be as nearly at right angles as is possible and in no case shall be less than sixty (60) degrees. The block corners at intersections shall be rounded at the curb line with a curve having a radius of not less than 20 feet.

(f) Street jogs with center line offsets of less than 125 feet shall be prohibited.

(g) When connecting street lines deflect from each other at any one point by more than 10 degrees and not more than 45 degrees, they shall be connected by a curve with a radius of as many feet as the Planning Board shall require to permit safe vision for operators of vehicles.

120

(h) All changes in grade shall be connected by vertical curves of sufficient radius to provide a smooth transition and proper sight distance.

(i) Dead-end streets, designed to be so permanently, shall be provided at the closed end with a turn around having an outside roadway diameter of at least 100 feet and a street property line diameter of at least 120 feet. The length of any dead-end street allowed shall require the approval of the Planning Board and the Township Committee.

If a dead-end street is of a temporary nature, a similar turn around shall be provided and provisions made for future extension of the street and reversion of the excess right-of-way to the adjoining properties.

(j) No street shall have a name which will duplicate or so nearly duplicate as to be confused with the names of existing streets. The continuation of an existing street shall have the same name.

3. *Blocks*

(a) Block length and width or acreage within bounding roads shall be such as to accommodate the size of lot required in the area by the zoning ordinance and to provide for convenient access, circulation control and safety of street traffic.

(b) In blocks over 1000 feet long, pedestrian cross walks may be required in locations deemed necessary by the Planning Board. Such walkway shall be 10 feet wide and be straight from street to street.

(c) For commercial, group housing or industrial use, block size shall be sufficient to meet all area and yard requirements for such use.

4. *Lots*

(a) Lot dimensions and area shall not be less than the requirements of the zoning ordinance.

(b) Insofar as is practical, side lot lines shall be at right angles to straight streets, and radial to curved streets.

(c) Each lot must front upon an approved street certified by the Township Committee as a suitable street, or in the case of new streets, on such streets as may be constructed in accordance with the provisions of Article VII, 1 (a).

(d) Where extra width has been dedicated for widening of existing streets, lots shall begin at such extra width line, and all set-backs shall be measured from such line.

(e) Where there is a question as to the suitability of a lot or lots for their intended use due to factors such as rock formations, flood conditions or similar circumstances, the Planning Board may, after adequate investigation withhold approval of such lots.

5. *Public Use and Service Areas*

In all developments of 20 residential lots or more. Community Facilities Areas shall be established of a total area equal to a minimum 20% of the net area of the residential lots excluding streets, provided however, that there shall be not more than 0.75 lots per acre of gross area of the tract, including streets.

Such areas may also be required for major residential subdivisions of less than 20 lots where considered appropriate by the Planning Board. Land for Township ownership will normally be restricted to that designated for community-wide use such as for school sites and major parks. Provision shall be made in the form of deed restrictions on the properties to be sold or by other means for the maintenance of the Community Facilities Areas by neighborhood associations or semi-public institutions providing local neighborhood services such as churches and parochial schools. Natural features such as trees, brooks, hill-tops and views shall be preserved wherever possible and incorporated in such Community Facilities Areas.

6. *Drainage Ways*

Where a subdivision is traversed by water course, drainage way, wet weather line of surface drainage, channel or stream, there should be provided a storm water easement or drainage right-of-way conforming substantially with the lines of such water course, and such further width of construction, or both, as will be adequate for the purpose. Such drainage ways shall be incorporated in the required Community Facilities Areas wherever possible.

7. *Electric and Gas Utilities*

For all major subdivision, other than those in an R-3 rural zone, electric, gas and telephone utility lines shall be installed underground. The applicant shall arrange with the serving utility for the underground installation of the utility's distribution supply facilities in accordance with the provisions of the applicable Standard Terms and Conditions incorporated as a part of its Tariff as the same are then on file with the State of New Jersey Board of Public Utility Commissioners and the applicant shall submit to the Planning Board prior to the granting of Final Approval a written instrument from each serving utility which shall evidence full compliance with the provisions of this paragraph.

8. *Reverse Frontage*

All lots in major subdivisions located on streets designated as Major Thoroughfares shall have reverse frontage with respect to such streets, i. e. shall front on other streets located away from such major thoroughfare. A 20 ft. transition strip shall be provided within the lot areas along Major Thoroughfares with plantings as required for transition strips in Commercial and Industrial Zones.

9. *Prevention of Excessive Similarity of Housing Design*

Excessive similarity of adjoining houses in building dimensions and construction materials, to such an extent as to impair the stability of future property values and encourage neighborhood deterioration, shall be avoided.

YORKTOWN, NEW YORK, CLUSTERING ORDINANCE (G)

WHEREAS, the Town is desirous of encouraging flexibility of design and development of land in such a manner as to promote the most appropriate use of lands, to facilitate the adequate and economical provisions of streets and utilities, and to preserve the natural and scenic qualities of open land, and

WHEREAS, the Town Board is cognizant of Section 281 of the Town Law, as amended, which generally provides for certain modifications of the Town's zoning provisions to attain such ends; and

WHEREAS, the Planning Board heretofore requested, and the Director of Planning have recommended, that authority to act under the statutes be granted to the Planning Board, and

WHEREAS, certain standards governing the use of this authority have been recommended by the Director of Planning.

NOW THEREFORE BE IT RESOLVED that said standards hereinafter designated as "Clustering Standards" and set forth below, be adopted, and be it

FURTHER RESOLVED, that authorization is hereby granted to the Planning Board, Town of Yorktown, N. Y., as hereinafter set forth and pursuant to Section 281 of the Town Law, as amended, to simultaneously with the approval of a plat modify applicable provisions of the Zoning Ordinance, subject to the conditions set forth by said Section 281, and further subject to the following standards and procedures:

1. Said authorization shall be applicable only for lands in R1-20 and R1-40 Districts for maximum permitted densities of 1.5 and 0.9 DU/acre respectively, and shall only be applied to single family detached residences under clustering standards adopted pursuant to this resolution.
2. Written application by an owner or agent for the use of the said clustering standards shall be made to the Planning Board. Said Board shall transmit such application to the Town Board with a request for authority to act in accordance with the said clustering standards.

CLUSTERING STANDARDS

Purpose—The purpose of these standards is to permit in existing residential districts, the clustering of single family houses on reduced sized lots and the grouping of the open space made available by this reduction so as to achieve a design of such development that will provide an alternate pattern of subdivision layout to the standard uniform lot and street pattern which prevails under the current zoning ordinance and subdivision regulations.

The standards set forth are designed to achieve:

1. A characteristic of design and site planning in which several houses are grouped together (clustered) on a tract of land and each cluster of houses serve as a module which is set off from others like it by an intervening space that helps give visual definition to each individual cluster.
2. The preservation of undeveloped land that is held for the common recreational enjoyment of the community residents or the Town at large.

Site Standards—

1. For a subdivision of single family dwellings containing five or more lots, the land upon which such dwellings are to be constructed shall have an area of not less than twenty (20) acres.

123

2. The site, when developed, shall be served by an approved common water supply system and an approved common sanitary sewer system.

3. The site shall have street frontage sufficient to construct the necessary major road or roads to service such development.

Lot Standards—

1. For individual single family dwellings or for a subdivision of single family dwellings containing 4 or less lots, each lot and building(s) thereon shall comply with the lot area, yard, and building standards of the zoned district.

2. For a subdivision of single family dwellings containing five or more lots in an R1-R20 District, each lot and buildings thereon shall comply with the lot area, yard and building standards of the R1-10 District.

3. For a subdivision of single family dwellings containing five or more lots in an R1-40 District, each lot and buildings thereon shall comply with the lot area, yard and dwelling standards of the R1-20 District.

4. For all other permitted uses, each site or lot for such use and the building(s) thereon shall comply with the lot area, yard, and building standards as specified for such use in the zoned district.

5. Dwellings and their individual lots shall be arranged to form groups or clusters within the site. The arrangement, size and location of the clusters on the site shall be approved by the Planning Board only if in their determination such arrangement, size and location will achieve the intent of the regulations and the purposes for which they have been set.

6. Major cul-de-sacs with widened turn arounds shall be designated by the Planning Board and shall be required to have 50 ft. R-O-W with 30 ft. pavement leading to turn around areas with 65 ft. radius, having a pavement radius of 45 ft. Other cul-de-sacs, or street access shall be as approved by Planning Board and shown on improvement plan.

Open Space Reservation, Regulation and Maintenance—

1. There shall be common open space(s) within any site, or portion thereof, which is submitted for final approval, and exclusive of the area(s) within any individual lots, which open space(s) shall have an area of at least 11,600 sq. ft. in an R1-20 District, and 23,200 sq. ft. in R1-40 District, for each dwelling (lot) within the site submitted. Such open space(s) shall be usable for recreational or other outdoor living purposes and for preserving large trees, tree groves, woods, ponds, streams, glens, rock outcrops, native plant life and wild life cover. The use of any open space may be further limited or controlled at the time of final plat approval where necessary to protect adjacent properties or uses.

2. The common open space(s) shall be shown on the subdivision plan and with appropriate notation on the face thereof to indicate that it
   a) shall not be used for future building lots.
   b) a part or all of the common open space may, at the Town's option, be accepted in dedication by the Town and operated as a Town Recreational facility.

3. a) If any or all of the common open space is to be reserved for use by the residents, the formation and incorporation by the developer of a neighborhood association shall be required prior to final plat approval.
   b) Covenants for mandatory membership in the association setting forth the owners rights and interest and privileges in the association and the

common land, shall be approved by the Planning Board and included in the deed for each lot.

c) This neighborhood association shall have the responsibility of maintaining the common open space(s) and operation and maintenance of local neighborhood recreational facilities within such open space(s).

d) The Association shall be empowered to levy annual charges against all property owners to defray the expenses connected with the maintenance of open spaces and neighborhood recreational facilities. Such charges shall become a lien against any property which may be in default.

e) The developer or subdivider shall maintain control of such open space(s) and be responsible for their maintenance until development sufficient to support the association has taken place or, alternately, the objectives of clustering have been met. Such determination shall be made by the Planning Board upon request of the Neighborhood Association or the developer or subdivider.

f) Prior to plat approval, the Town shall form a Park District of the lands within the site which district shall have the power to take over the work of the neighborhood association in the event of default of such association, and to tax the property owners of such district in order to defray cost.

Required Plans and Procedures:

1. An applicant for Clustering Development under these standards shall file with the Planning Board the application and plans required for subdivision review and approval as set forth in the Town Land Subdivision Regulations. Such application and plans shall have clearly marked upon their face that said plan is for Clustering Development in accordance with these standards and the requirements of the Town Land Subdivision Regulations.

2. The developer, at the time of application will submit a preliminary subdivision layout conforming in all respects to a layout developed on a straight R1-20 or R1-40 basis, and having no lots smaller than 20,000 sq. ft. or 40,000 sq. ft. respectively. Such layout shall be reviewed by the Planning Board to ascertain compliance with the existing regulations and will be utilized to set the maximum number of dwelling units to be allowed by clustering. (Normally in one family residential subdivisions, slopes greater than 20% grade or low, wet, marshy or swampy lands are not considered buildable lands and, therefore, will not be allowed in the computation for allowable number of dwelling units.)

3. The clustering subdivision plan shall be examined and evaluated in terms of the statement of purpose and shall be approved after a determination has been made that the proposed subdivision best meets the ends sought. This review and approval shall be made by the Town Planning Board.

4. The developer shall be required to submit profile studies of all difficult building plots to ascertain that the plan will not develop radical topographical changes in either the road or plot areas, and that the plots will have usable and safe access to the open space areas.

5. As part of the required public hearing, the notice of hearing shall indicate the number of lots, amount of open space, and dwelling unit density of the proposed subdivision.

6. Any plan for Clustering Development shall not be approved by the Planning Board unless the same complies with all of these standards and the

(G) requirements of the Land Subdivision Regulations. In approving such development, the Planning Board shall require such conditions as are deemed necessary to preserve and protect the open spaces therein from any encroachment by future building or uses not shown on the plan at the time of approval, or subsequent amendment thereof.

Dated: April 4th, 1967

NEW YORK GENERAL MUNICIPAL LAW, SECTION 281, "CLUSTER ENABLING ACT"

Section 281 of the town law. Approval of plats; conditions for changes in zoning provisions. The town board is hereby empowered by resolution to authorize the planning board, simultaneously with the approval of a plat or plats pursuant to this article, to modify applicable provisions of the zoning ordinance, subject to the conditions hereinafter set forth and such other reasonable conditions as the town board may in its discretion add thereto. Such authorization shall specify the lands outside the limits of any incorporated village to which this procedure may be applicable. The purposes of such authorization shall be to enable and encourage flexibility of design and development of land in such a manner as to promote the most appropriate use of land, to facilitate the adequate and economical provision of streets and utilities, and to preserve the natural and scenic qualities of open lands. The conditions hereinabove referred to are as follows:

(a) If the owner makes written application for the use of this procedure, it may be followed at the discretion of the planning board if, in said board's judgment, its application would benefit the town.

(b) This procedure shall be applicable only to lands zoned for residential purposes, and its application shall result in a permitted number of dwelling units which shall in no case exceed the number which could be permitted, in the planning board's judgment, if the land were subdivided into lots conforming to the minimum lot size and density requirements of the zoning ordinance applicable to the district or districts in which such land is situated and conforming to all other applicable requirements.

(c) The dwelling units permitted may be, at the discretion of the planning board and subject to the conditions set forth by the town board, in detached, semi-detached, attached, or multi-story structures.

(d) In the event that the application of this procedure results in a plat showing lands available for park, recreation, open space, or other municipal purposes directly related to the plat, then the planning board as a condition of plat approval may establish such conditions on the ownership, use, and maintenance of such lands as it deems necessary to assure the preservation of such lands for their intended purposes. The town board may require that such conditions shall be approved by the town board before the plat may be approved for filing.

(e) The proposed site plan, including areas within which structures may be located, the height and spacing of buildings, open spaces and their landscaping, off-street open and enclosed parking spaces, and streets, driveways and all other physical features as shown on said plan or otherwise described, accompanied by a statement setting forth the nature of such modifications, changes, or supplements of existing zoning provisions as are not shown on said site plan, shall be subject to review and public hearing by the planning board in the same manner as set forth in sections two hundred seventy-six and two hundred seventy-seven of this article for the approval of plats.

(f) On the filing of the plat in the office of the county clerk or register, a copy shall be filed with the town clerk, who shall make appropriate notations and references thereto in the town zoning ordinance or map.

(Chapter 963, Laws of 1963)   127

ASPETUCK LAND TRUST, INC.
CERTIFICATE OF INCORPORATION

We, the incorporators, certify that we hereby associate ourselves as a body politic and corporate under the Nonstock Corporate Act of the State of Connecticut.

1. The name of the Corporation is: ASPETUCK LAND TRUST, INC.

2. The nature of the activities to be conducted, or the purposes to be promoted or carried out by the corporation, are as follows:

(a) To engage in and otherwise promote for the benefit of the general public the preservation of natural resources of the State of Connecticut, including water resources, marshland, swamps, woodland and open spaces, and the plant and animal life therein and the preservation of unique historic and scenic sites;

(b) To engage in and otherwise promote the scientific study of and to educate the public regarding local natural resources including plants, animals, birds and other wildlife;

(c) To acquire, by gift, purchase or otherwise, real and personal property, both tangible and intangible, of every sort and description and to use such property in such manner as the directors of the corporation shall deem appropriate to carry out such purposes;

(d) To use all property held or controlled by this corporation and the net earnings thereof in the United States of America for the benefit of all the inhabitants of the State of Connecticut for the conservational, educational and scientific purposes for which the corporation is formed as set forth in this Article;

(e) In connection with the foregoing to do any and all things permitted by the Statutes of the State of Connecticut.

3. No part of the corporation's income is distributable to its members, directors or officers and the corporation shall not have or issue shares of stock or pay dividends.

4. The classes, the manner of election or appointment and the qualifications and rights of the members of each class, are as follows:

There shall be two classes of members; regular members and special gift members.

Regular members shall include those persons who have completed and submitted to the secretary a form of application to be determined from time to time by the Board of Directors and have paid dues as prescribed by the Board of Directors.

Special gift members shall include those persons who have conveyed by gift a minimum of one acre of land or an equivalent amount of money as determined from time to time in the By-Laws.

Any member may be expelled from the corporation upon recommendation of the Board of Directors and a vote of two-thirds of the members present and voting at any regular or special meeting of the corporation. Any membership shall be terminated upon the delinquency of payment of dues for a period in excess of two years unless such payment is specifically excused by the Board of Directors. All members shall be entitled to vote on any matter referred to the members by force of law or by act of the Board of Directors for decision. No member may vote by proxy or otherwise delegate his right to vote. Members shall annually elect directors to manage the affairs of the corporation.

5. The duration of the corporation shall be unlimited.

6. No part of the activities of the corporation shall consist of carrying on a propaganda, or otherwise attempting, to influence legislation, or participating in or intervening in, including the publishing or distributing of statements, any political campaign on behalf of any candidate for public office.

7. Upon the termination and liquidation of this corporation, all land and other assets owned by the corporation after payment of all obligations, shall be given to The Nature Conservancy, Washington, D. C. or similar organization.

(J)

FROM A NASSAU COUNTY, NEW YORK, AGREEMENT WITH A PRIVATE LANDOWNER FOR TRANSFER OF OPEN SPACE LAND

WITNESSETH:

WHEREAS, the party of the second part is the owner of the premises located in the Incorporated Village of Muttontown, Nassau County, New York, shown on the attached survey and more particularly described in Schedule A annexed hereto, together with the buildings and improvements thereon, consisting of approximately ninety-four acres having access to both Muttontown Lane and Route 25-A (said premises being hereinafter referred to as the "premises"); and

WHEREAS, the party of the second part wishes to convey easements over or convey the premises or parts thereof to the party of the first part as a means of preserving the premises, or parts thereof, in their natural state and complying with the public policy of the State of New York in regard to the preservation of open spaces and areas, as expressed in Section 247 of the General Municipal Law of the State of New York;

NOW, THEREFORE, the parties mutually agree as follows:

1. The party of the second part hereby gives unto the party of the first part a license to use as a Nature Center, and no other purpose, that part of the premises consisting of approximately forty-eight acres more particularly described in Schedule B annexed hereto (said part being hereinafter referred to as the "licensed premises"), said license to be revocable upon sixty days notice in writing from the party of the second part to the party of the first part.

2. The party of the first part shall pay to the party of the second part a license fee of $1.00 per year.

3. The party of the second part, within thirty days after the approval of this agreement by the Board of Supervisors of Nassau County, as provided by Article 10 hereof, will deliver as a gift to the party of the first part and dedication for public purposes a bargain and sale deed, without covenants against grantor's acts, to not less than ten acres of the licensed premises, said easement or said deed to include that part of the licensed premises having access to Muttontown Lane.

4. The party of the first part upon the delivery of the deed as provided by Article 3 undertakes to commence promptly a Nature Center under professional direction to encourage the study of nature by children living in surrounding areas in Nassau County, such encouragement to include organized visits to the donated and licensed premises and walks through the same. The party of the first part will utilize for such Nature Center the licensed premises.

5. The party of the first part will construct no buildings on the licensed premises during the lifetime of the party of the second part without her prior approval in writing, which she shall be under no obligation to give, and such buildings shall in all events be limited to buildings required in connection with the Nature Center.

6. The party of the second part undertakes and agrees to convey and deliver to the County of Nassau at least forty acres of the premises described in Schedule B to be selected by her in her absolute discretion. The party of the second part shall have the right to make such conveyances from time to

130

time during her lifetime but no later than 1975 or by her will. The party of the second part shall also have the right to convey a permanent easement over any part of the licensed premises prior to a conveyance of the fee to such part. A survey of that part of the premises to be conveyed to the party of the first part in fee or by easement will promptly be furnished to the party of the second part upon her request. The party of the first part shall within thirty days after each conveyance in fee or easement or after the probate of her will in the State of New York accept such conveyance or devise by resolution of the Board of Supervisors and approval of the County Executive.

7. The party of the first part further agrees to accept a gift by the party of the second part of any easement over any part of the premises, or any conveyance of any part of the premises including any buildings thereon, which the party of the second part is willing to convey, either during her life or by the provisions of her will, and whether or not in fee or subject to the life estate of the party of the second part, provided the real property included in any such deed will be contiguous to property described in a previous deed to the party of the first part. The party of the first part agrees that it will hold all of the licensed premises for use as a Nature Center and the main residence and any part or all of the premises other than the licensed premises for a museum and for park purposes in connection with the museum, all such property to be held for such purposes for twenty years after the death of the party of the second part unless the approval to a change in use is given by the party of the second part during her life or her legal representatives after her death. The party of the first part will receive any property, whether the licensed premises or not, subject to the obligations to preserve the same, in the condition when conveyed and will preserve the open spaces and areas on the premises in accordance with the provisions of Section 247 of the General Municipal Law. Subject to the foregoing the party of the first part agrees that any conveyance pursuant to this agreement shall be held by it in perpetuity as a public trust for use as a public park by residents of the County of Nassau and that no buildings shall be erected thereon that will interfere with the obligation to preserve the premises and the open spaces and areas.

8. In the event of a breach of the provisions of this agreement and a failure by the party of the first part to correct the same within sixty days after notice from the party of the second part of such breach, the party of the second part may revoke this license and all rights of the party of the first part hereunder in regard to the licensed premises shall thereupon terminate, but despite such termination the party of the first part shall not be relieved of any obligations set forth herein in regard to any easement or deed conveyed to the party of the first part by the party of the second part in accordance with this agreement.

9. The party of the second part will pay all real estate taxes so long as the fee is retained by her, but the party of the first part will cooperate to the extent legally permissible to have the assessments thereon take into consideration the limitation on future use of the land, as provided by Section 247 of the General Municipal Law. The party of the first part will take appropriate action to see that no damages are caused to the trees, bushes or other natural objects located on the licensed premises and will provide adequate police protection to maintain order thereon and to prevent trespassing therefrom on other property of the party of the second part. The party of the first part will be solely responsible for the preservation and regulation of the licensed   131

(J)

premises and undertakes and agrees to fence the same at its sole expense. The party of the first part hereby undertakes and agrees to indemnify and hold harmless the party of the second part from and against any and all liabilities and damages and any and all suits, claims and demands of every kind and nature, including reasonable counsel fees, by or on behalf of any person, firm, association or corporation, arising out of the occupation of the premises by the party of the first part, including, but not by way of limitation of the generality of the foregoing, any and all suits, claims, demands, liabilities and damages arising out of or based upon any accident, injury or damage, however occurring, which shall or may happen on or about the premises, and from or against any matter or thing growing out of the condition, maintenance, repair, alteration, use, occupation or operation of the premises or the streets, sidewalks or curbs in front of or adjacent thereto.

10. The provisions of this agreement are dependent upon approval of the same on or before December 31, 1964, by the Board of Supervisors, Nassau County and the adoption by said Board of a resolution implementing the same.

11. Any notice under the provisions of this agreement shall be given by registered mail directed as follows:

To party of the first part: To party of the second part:
Nassau County Executive Building
West Street
Mineola, New York

12. The party of the first part shall permit the party of the second part or her agents to enter upon the licensed premises at all reasonable times to inspect the same, and to take such action as is necessary to preserve the trees, shrubs and other natural objects and to plant replacements or to make additional plantings to beautify the licensed premises, all at the expense of the party of the second part.

13. The license is not assignable under any conditions.

14. In the operation of the Nature Center the party of the first part will consult with the party of the second part and make every reasonable effort to operate the same in accordance with the wishes and intent of the party of the second part. In no event shall the operation of the same interfere with the enjoyment by the party of the second part of the adjoining property as a residence. The use of the Nature Center should be limited to daylight hours, except with the express consent of the party of the second part.

15. The giving to the party of the first part of an easement over part or all of the licensed premises shall not in any way affect the rights or obligations of the parties under this agreement.

132

FROM A COVENANT INVOLVING THE NATURE CONSERVANCY, INC. AND PRIVATE LANDOWNERS ON THE BANTAM RIVER

(K)

WITNESSETH:

WHEREAS, the parties hereto are owners of land adjacent to and abutting upon the Bantam River in said Town of Litchfield; and

WHEREAS, the banks of the Bantam River and the land adjacent thereto in the area where the properties of the parties hereto are situated are of rare natural beauty and their terrain, vegetation, and wildlife have not yet been spoiled by the activities of mankind; and

WHEREAS, the parties hereto are mindful of the dwindling number of regions where nature has been allowed to develop her own plan, uninfluenced and undisturbed by the activities of mankind; and

WHEREAS, the parties hereto are desirous of conserving this area, as nearly as may be practicable, in its present state in order to preserve its natural beauty both for this generation and future generations; and

WHEREAS, other owners of land adjacent to and abutting upon the Bantam River have entered, or it is contemplated that they will enter, into agreements with THE NATURE CONSERVANCY OF CONNECTICUT, INC. containing covenants in whole or in part identical with or similar to those contained herein;

NOW, THEREFORE, the parties hereto for and in consideration of the mutual covenants herein set forth, each on behalf of himself, his heirs, executors, administrators, successors, and assigns agree with the others and with their respective heirs, executors, administrators, successors, and assigns that the following shall be covenants running with the land described in Appendix A attached hereto and hereby made a part hereof, and that the same shall be enforceable by the parties hereto and each of them and by their respective heirs, executors, administrators, successors, and assigns, and any of them and by any other owners (and by the successors in title of such owners) of land adjacent to and abutting upon the Bantam River who have heretofore entered or may hereafter enter into covenants in whole or in part identical with or similar to those hereinafter contained, in regard to so much of such land as lies within   feet of the nearer bank of said Bantam River bounding said property (or if said property is on both sides of said river, then within   feet of each of said banks):

No sewage, industrial waste, or other objectionable or offensive material shall be dumped or discharged into said river upon, over, or from such land, in so far as the owner thereof can control the same, nor shall said area be used for leaching or for any sewage disposal field;

No billboards or other outdoor advertising signs shall be erected thereon;

No topsoil shall be removed therefrom;

No commercial lumbering operations shall be conducted thereon;

No sand, gravel, or other minerals shall be excavated therefrom;

No pig pens, slaughter houses, or other structures for the conduct of activities that would be considered a nuisance if conducted in a residential area shall be erected thereon;

No trees shall be cut thereon unless dead, diseased, or decayed or for the better landscaping of the area, or for the improvement of the existing growth;   133

(K)

No roadways shall be constructed, nor shall any existing roadway be substantially altered;

No consent shall be given to the installation or extension of any public utility facilities;

No buildings of any description shall be erected thereon;

There shall be no dumping or burning of refuse thereon;

There shall be no hunting or trapping thereon;

There shall be no stripping of the land in such a way as to contribute to the erosion thereof.

A MODEL "STREAM EASEMENT" PROPOSED BY THE OPEN SPACE ACTION INSTITUTE IN WESTCHESTER COUNTY, NEW YORK

THIS INDENTURE, made this   day of   , 19   , by and between   residing at
, party of the first part, and WESTCHESTER COUNTY, a municipal corporation of the State of New York, with an office at   , party of the second part.

WITNESSETH:

WHEREAS, the party of the first part is the owner of premises adjacent to and bordering on   Creek in the Town of   , Westchester County, New York, described in Schedule A hereto annexed, hereinafter referred to as "the Premises," and

WHEREAS, the party of the first part and other owners of land adjacent to and bordering upon the said   Creek desire to preserve, maintain and enhance the natural beauty, vegetation, wild life and other natural and scenic resources of the area and to protect the area from future urban development, and

WHEREAS, Section 247 of the General Municipal Law of New York provides for the acquisition by any county, city, town or village of interests or rights in real property for the preservation of open spaces, including the acquisition of any development right, easement, covenant or other contractual right with respect to land within such municipality to achieve the purposes therein set forth;

NOW, THEREFORE, in consideration of One Dollar and other good and valuable consideration paid by the party of the second part to the party of the first part, the receipt of which is hereby acknowledged, the party of the first part does hereby grant, transfer and convey to the party of the second part, a scenic and conservation easement with respect to the Premises, to have and to hold said easement, right and interest with respect to the Premises unto the party of the second part, its successors and assigns forever, for the benefit of the public, reserving to the party of the first part, his heirs, personal representatives and assigns, the exclusive right of occupancy and use of the Premises, subject to the conditions, covenants and agreements hereinafter set forth, which shall constitute a servitude upon and with respect to the Premises.

The party of the first part, on behalf of himself, his heirs, personal representatives and assigns, covenants and agrees as follows:

1. The Premises will forever be kept open and free of all buildings or other structures, including any billboards or other advertising signs, except as hereinafter set forth.

2. No sewage, industrial waste or other objectionable or offensive material or refuse shall be permitted to be discharged into
Creek from the Premises, nor shall any portion of the Premises bordering said creek be used for leeching or for a sewage disposal field, and no dumping or burning of refuse shall be permitted on the Premises.

3. No dam shall be constructed in any part of   Creek within or abutting the Premises.

135

(L)

4. The natural resources of the Premises shall remain undisturbed and to this end no top soil, sand, gravel, rock or minerals shall be excavated or removed therefrom, and nothing shall be permitted to occur on the Premises which would contribute to the erosion of the land, and no commercial lumbering operations shall be permitted on the Premises, and no trees shall be cut or removed, and no other plants or vegetation shall be destroyed or removed, except for the removal of such dead, diseased or decayed trees or vegetation which may be required for conservation or scenic purposes.

5. No building or structure on the Premises nor any part of the Premises shall be used for the conduct of any dangerous, offensive or noxious trading, business or occupation nor for any use that would constitute a nuisance if it occurred in a residential area.

6. No roadway nor any facility of any public utility other than existing roadways and public utility facilities shall be permitted to be constructed or installed on the Premises, and no existing roadway or public utility facility shall be enlarged or extended on the Premises.

7. No hunting or trapping shall be permitted on the Premises.

The party of the first part reserves the right to maintain, repair and improve and to replace and reconstruct any existing buildings, structures, roadways or other facilities now existing on the Premises without, however, enlarging or extending any of them. The party of the first part further reserves the right to the exclusive use of the Premises and all buildings, structures and facilities thereon insofar as such use is not inconsistent with the covenants and agreements hereinabove set forth, and the party of the first part may exclude the general public or any person or persons from the use of the Premises.

The party of the second part agrees that while the valuation placed upon the Premises for real estate tax purposes must, in accordance with Section 247 of the General Municipal Law, take into account the limitation on the future use of the land, nevertheless, if, at any time, the Premises shall be condemned by the party of the second part or by any municipality or state or governmental body, then the easement hereby granted shall terminate and all rights and interests in the Premises hereby granted shall revert to the party of the first part, his heirs, personal representatives or assigns, so that as of the time of such condemnation the Premises shall not be subject to the limitation of such easement.

The party of the second part hereby accepts the foregoing grant of easement and the parties hereto agree that the covenants, agreements, conditions and restrictions hereinabove set forth shall in all respects be binding upon the parties hereto, their heirs, personal representatives, successors and assigns.

IN WITNESS WHEREOF, the party of the first part has duly executed this agreement, and the party of the second part has caused this agreement to be executed on its behalf by its duly authorized officer and its corporate seal to be hereunto affixed, the day and year first above written.

....

WESTCHESTER COUNTY

136

By ....

FROM AN OPEN SPACE EASEMENT IN OYSTER BAY, LONG ISLAND (VILLAGE OF COVE NECK)

party of the second part,

WITNESSETH, that the party of the first part, in consideration of the acceptance by the party of the second part of the unconditional gift of the development rights to, and the open space or scenic easement over, the premises described below

does hereby grant and release unto the party of the second part, its successors and assigns forever, in perpetuity, the right to construct any structures, sign, fence or other improvement on the following described premises to alter the contours thereof and to plant or remove flora thereon so that the same shall be burdened by an open space or scenic easement and shall be preserved as, and forever remain, an open space or open area and shall forever be so maintained in order that the natural scenic beauty thereof shall be conserved for the benefit of the public, to wit:

ALL that certain plot, piece or parcel of land, situate, lying and being in the Incorporated Village of Cove Neck, Town of Oyster Bay, County of Nassau and State of New York, bounded and described as follows:

(Description omitted)

THIS DEED is only for the development rights to, and an open space or scenic easement over, the above described premises; the party of the first part is retaining the fee title to these premises and all incidents of ownership therein except the right to construct any structure, sign, fence or other improvement thereon, to alter the contours thereof and to plant or remove flora thereon; and this deed is delivered by the party of the first part and accepted by the party of the second part pursuant to the authority contained in Section 247 of the General Municipal Law of the State of New York and it shall be construed in accordance with the intent and purposes of that Section.

TO HAVE AND TO HOLD the development rights to, and an open space or scenic easement over, the above described premises, herein granted, unto the party of the second part, its successors and assigns forever.

While there was no monetary consideration for this conveyance, the in compliance with Section 13 of the Lien Law, covenants that the grantor will receive the consideration for this conveyance and will hold the right to receive such consideration as a trust fund to be applied first for the purpose of paying the cost of the improvement and that the grantor will apply the same first to the payment of the cost of the improvement before using any part of the total of the same for any other purpose.

137

NEW JERSEY FARMLAND ASSESSMENT ACT

(Chapter 48, L. 1964; Approved May 11, 1964)

An Act concerning the valuation, assessment and taxation of land actively devoted to agricultural or horticultural uses; defining such uses; providing for penalties and tax lien; supplementing Title 54 of the Revised Statutes; and making an appropriation.

WHEREAS, On November 5, 1963 an amended Article VIII, Section 1, paragraph 1 of the Constitution was duly adopted and became effective on December 5, 1963; and

WHEREAS, By said amendment it was provided that the Legislature shall enact laws to provide that the value of land, not less than 5 acres in area, which is determined by the assessing officer of the taxing jurisdiction to be actively devoted to agricultural or horticultural use, and to have been so devoted for at least 2 successive years immediately preceding the tax year in issue, shall for local tax purposes, on application of the owner, be that value which such land has for agricultural or horticultural use; and

WHEREAS, Said Constitutional Amendment further provided that any such laws shall provide that when land which has been valued in this manner for local tax purposes is applied to a use other than for agricultural or horticultural it shall be subject to additional taxes as provided in said amendment; and

WHEREAS, It was further provided by said amendment that such laws shall provide for the equalization of assessments of land valued in accordance with the said provisions of said amendment and for the assessment and collection of any additional taxes levied thereupon and shall include such other provisions as shall be necessary to carry out the provisions of said amendment; now, therefore,

BE IT ENACTED by the Senate and General Assembly of the State of New Jersey:

1. This act shall be known and referred to by its short title, the "Farmland Assessment Act of 1964."

2. For general property tax purposes, the value of land, not less than 5 acres in area, which is actively devoted to agricultural or horticultural use and which has been so devoted for at least the 2 successive years immediately preceding the tax year in issue, shall, on application of the owner, and approval thereof as hereinafter provided, be that value which such land has for agricultural or horticultural use.

3. Land shall be deemed to be in agricultural use when devoted to the production for sale of plants and animals useful to man, including but not limited to: forages and sod crops; grains and feed crops; dairy animals and dairy products; poultry and poultry products; livestock, including beef cattle, sheep, swine, horses, ponies, mules or goats, including the breeding and grazing of any or all of such animals; bees and apiary products; fur animals; trees and forest products; or when devoted to and meeting the requirements and qualifications for payments or other compensation pursuant to a soil conservation program under an agreement with an agency of the federal government.

4. Land shall be deemed to be in horticultural use when devoted to the production for sale of fruits of all kinds, including grapes, nuts and berries; vegetables; nursery, floral, ornamental and greenhouse products; or when

devoted to and meeting the requirements and qualifications for payments or other compensation pursuant to a soil conservation program under an agreement with an agency of the federal government.

5. Land shall be deemed to be actively devoted to agricultural or horticultural use when the gross sales of agricultural or horticultural products produced thereon together with any payments received under a soil conservation program have averaged at least $500 per year during the 2-year period immediately preceding the tax year in issue, or there is clear evidence of anticipated yearly gross sales and such payments amounting to at least $500 within a reasonable period of time.

6. Land which is actively devoted to agricultural or horticultural use shall be eligible for valuation, assessment and taxation as herein provided when it meets the following qualifications:

(a) It has been so devoted for at least the 2 successive years immediately preceding the tax year for which valuation under this act is requested;

(b) The area of such land is not less than 5 acres when measured in accordance with the provisions of section 11 hereof; and

(c) Application by the owner of such land for valuation hereunder is submitted on or before October 1 of the year immediately preceding the tax year to the assessor of the taxing district in which such land is situated on the form prescribed by the Director of the Division of Taxation.

(7) The assessor in valuing land which qualifies as land actively devoted to agricultural or horticultural use under the tests prescribed by this act, and as to which the owner thereof has made timely application for valuation, assessment and taxation hereunder for the tax year in issue, shall consider only those indicia of value which such land has for agricultural or horticultural use. In addition to use of his personal knowledge, judgment and experience as to the value of land in agricultural or horticultural use, he shall, in arriving at the value of such land, consider available evidence of agricultural and horticultural capability derived from the soil survey data at Rutgers—The State University, the National Cooperative Soil Survey, and the recommendations of value of such land as made by any county or State-wide committee which may be established to assist the assessor.

8. When land which is in agricultural or horticultural use and is being valued, assessed and taxed under the provisions of this act, is applied to a use other than agricultural or horticultural, it shall be subject to additional taxes hereinafter referred to as roll-back taxes, in an amount equal to the difference, if any, between the taxes paid or payable on the basis of the valuation and the assessment authorized hereunder and the taxes that would have been paid or payable had the land been valued, assessed and taxed as other land in the taxing district, in the current tax year (the year of change in use) and in such of the two tax years immediately preceding, in which the land was valued, assessed and taxed as herein provided.

If in the tax year in which a change in use of the land occurs, the land was not valued, assessed and taxed under this act, then such land shall be subject to rollback taxes for such of the two tax years, immediately preceding, in which the land was valued, assessed and taxed hereunder.

In determining the amounts of the rollback taxes chargeable on land which has undergone a change in use, the assessor shall for each of the rollback tax years involved, ascertain:

(a) The full and fair value of such land under the valuation standard applicable to other land in the taxing district;

(b) The amount of the land assessment for the particular tax year by multiplying such full and fair value by the average real property assessment ratio of the taxing district, as determined by the county board of taxation for the purposes of the county equalization table for such year, pursuant to sections 54:3-17 to 19 of the Revised Statutes:

(c) The amount of the additional assessment on the land for the particular tax year by deducting the amount of the actual assessment on the land for that year from the amount of the land assessment determined under (b) hereof; and

(d) The amount of the rollback tax for that tax year by multiplying the amount of the additional assessment determined under (c) hereof by the general property tax rate of the taxing district applicable for that tax year.

9. The assessment, collection, apportionment and payment over of the rollback taxes imposed by section 8, the attachment of the lien for such taxes, and the right of a taxing district, owner or other interested party to review any judgment of the county board of taxation affecting such rollback taxes, shall be governed by the procedures provided for the assessment and taxation of omitted property under Chapter 413 of the Laws of 1947. Such procedures shall apply to each tax year for which rollback taxes may be imposed, notwithstanding the limitation prescribed in section 1 of said chapter respecting the periods for which omitted property assessments may be imposed.

10. The Director of the Division of Taxation in equalizing the value of land assessed and taxed under this act for the purposes of State school aid, and each county board of taxation in equalizing such land for the purposes of determining the "apportionment valuation" under section 54:4-49 of the Revised Statutes, shall determine the true value of such land on the basis of its agricultural or horticultural use. The director shall promulgate rules and regulations to effectuate the purposes of this section.

11. In determining the total area of land actively devoted to agricultural or horticultural use there shall be included the area of all land under barns, sheds, silos, cribs, greenhouses and like structures, lakes, dams, ponds, streams, irrigation ditches and like facilities, but land under and such additional land as may be actually used in connection with the farmhouse shall be excluded in determining such total area.

12. All structures, which are located on land in agricultural or horticultural use and the farmhouse and the land on which the farmhouse is located, together with the additional land used in connection therewith, shall be valued, assessed and taxed by the same standards, methods and procedures as other taxable structures and other land in the taxing district.

13. Eligibility of land for valuation, assessment and taxation under this act shall be determined for each tax year separately.

Application shall be submitted by the owner to the assessor of the taxing district in which such land is situated on or before October 1 of the year immediately preceding the tax year for which such valuation, assessment and taxation are sought. An application once filed with the assessor for the ensuing tax year may not be withdrawn by the applicant after October 1 of the pretax year.

If a change in use of the land occurs between October 1 and December 31 of the pre-tax year, either the assessor or the county board of taxation shall deny or nullify such application and, after examination and inquiry, shall determine the full and fair value of said land under the valuation standard applicable to other land in the taxing district and shall assess the same according to such value. If, notwithstanding such change of use, the land is valued, assessed and taxed under the provisions of this act in the ensuing year, the assessor shall enter an assessment, as an added assessment against such land, in the "Added Assessment List" for the particular year involved in the manner prescribed in Chapter 397 of the Laws of 1941. The amount of the added assessment shall be in an amount equal to the difference, if any, between the assessment imposed under this act and the assessment which would have been imposed had the land been valued and assessed as other land in the taxing district. The enforcement and collection of additional taxes resulting from any additional assessment so imposed shall be as provided by said chapter. The additional assessment imposed under this section shall not affect the rollback taxes, if any, under section 8 of this act.

14. Application for valuation, assessment and taxation of land in agricultural or horticultural use under this act shall be on a form prescribed by the Director of the Division of Taxation, and provided for the use of claimants by the governing bodies of the respective taxing districts. The form of application shall provide for the reporting of information pertinent to the provisions of Article VIII, Section 1, paragraph 1 (b) of the Constitution, as amended, and this act. A certification by the land owner that the facts set forth in the application are true may be prescribed by the director to be in lieu of a sworn statement to that effect. Statements so certified shall be considered as if made under oath and subject to the same penalties as provided by law for perjury.

15. Continuance of valuation, assessment and taxation under this act shall depend upon continuance of the land in agricultural or horticultural use and compliance with the other requirements of this act and not upon continuance in the same owner of title to the land. Liability to the rollback tax shall attach when a change in use of the land occurs but not when a change in ownership of the title takes place if the new owner continues the land in agricultural or horticultural use, under the conditions prescribed in this act.

16. Separation or split off of a part of the land which is being valued, assessed and taxed under this act, either by conveyance or other action of the owner of such land, for a use other than agricultural or horticultural, shall subject the land so separated to liability for the rollback taxes applicable thereto, but shall not impair the right of the remaining land to continuance of valuation, assessment and taxation hereunder, provided it meets the 5-acre minimum requirement and such other conditions of this act as may be applicable.

17. The taking of land which is being valued, assessed and taxed under this act by right of eminent domain shall not subject the land so taken to the rollback taxes herein imposed.

18. Where contiguous land in agricultural or horticultural use in one ownership is located in more than one taxing district, compliance with the 5-acre minimum area requirement shall be determined on the basis of the total area of such land and not the area which is located in the particular taxing district.

19. The factual details to be shown on the assessor's tax list and duplicate with respect to land which is being valued, assessed and taxed under this act

141

shall be the same as those set forth by the assessor with respect to other taxable property in the taxing district.

20. There is hereby created a State Farmland Evaluation Advisory Committee, the members of which shall be the Director of the Division of Taxation; the Dean of the College of Agriculture, Rutgers—The State University; and the Secretary of Agriculture. The Committee shall meet from time to time on the call of the Secretary of Agriculture and annually determine and publish a range of values for each of the several classifications of land in agricultural and horticultural use in the various areas of the State. The primary objective of the Committee shall be the determination of the ranges in fair value of such land based upon its productive capabilities when devoted to agricultural or horticultural uses. In making these annual determinations of value, the Committee shall consider available evidence of agricultural or horticultural capability derived from the soil survey at Rutgers—The State University, the National Cooperative Soil Survey, and such other evidence of value of land devoted exclusively to agricultural or horticultural uses as it may in its judgment deem pertinent. On or before October 1 of each year, the Committee shall make these ranges of fair value available to the assessing authority in each of the taxing districts in which land in agricultural and horticultural use is located.

21. The Director is empowered to promulgate such rules and regulations and to prescribe such forms as he shall deem necessary to effectuate the purposes of this act.

22. If any clause, sentence, subdivision, paragraph, section or part of this act be adjudged by any court of competent jurisdiction to be invalid, such judgment shall not affect, impair or invalidate the remainder thereof, but shall be confined in its operation to the clause, sentence, subdivision, paragraph, section or part thereof directly involved in the controversy in which said judgment shall have been rendered.

23. The sum of $50,000 is hereby appropriated to the Division of Taxation in the Department of the Treasury for the administration of this act for the period beginning on the effective date of this act and ending June 30, 1965, in addition to such other sums as may be appropriated to said Division.

24. The tax year 1965 shall be deemed to be the first tax year to which the provisions of this act shall apply, and this act shall apply to the tax year 1965 and subsequent tax years.

25. This act shall take effect immediately.

CONNECTICUT "ASSESSMENT" ACT

PUBLIC ACT NO. 490

AN ACT CONCERNING THE TAXATION AND PRESERVATION OF FARM, FOREST AND OPEN SPACE LAND.

Be it enacted by the Senate and House of Representatives in General Assembly convened:

SECTION 1. It is hereby declared (a) that it is in the public interest to encourage the preservation of farm land, forest land and open space land in order to maintain a readily available source of food and farm products close to the metropolitan areas of the state, to conserve the state's natural resources and to provide for the welfare and happiness of the inhabitants of the state, (b) that it is in the public interest to prevent the forced conversion of farm land, forest land and open space land to more intensive uses as the result of economic pressures caused by the assessment thereof for purposes of property taxation at values incompatible with their preservation as such farm land, forest land and open space land, and (c) that the necessity in the public interest of the enactment of the provisions of this act is a matter of legislative determination.

SEC. 2. When used in this act (a) the term "farm land" means any tract or tracts of land, including wood-land and wasteland, constituting a farm unit; (b) the term "forest land" means any tract or tracts of land aggregating twenty-five acres or more in area bearing tree growth in such quantity and so spaced as to constitute in the opinion of the state forester a forest area and maintained in the opinion of the state forester in a state of proper forest condition, (c) the term "open space land" means any area of land, including forest land and not excluding farm land, the preservation or restriction of the use of which would (1) maintain and enhance the conservation of natural or scenic resources, (2) protect natural streams or water supply, (3) promote conservation of soils, wetlands, beaches or tidal marshes, (4) enhance the value to the public of abutting or neighboring parks, forests, wildlife preserves, nature reservations or sanctuaries or other open spaces, (5) enhance public recreation opportunities, (6) preserve historic sites, or (7) promote orderly urban or suburban development; (d) the word "municipality" means any town, consolidated town and city, or consolidated town and borough; (e) the term "planning commission" means a planning commission created pursuant to section 8-19 of the 1961 supplement to the general statutes; (f) the term "plan of development" means a plan of development, including any amendment thereto, prepared or adopted pursuant to section 8-23 of said supplement.

SEC. 3. (a) An owner of land may apply for its classification as farm land an any assessment list of a municipality by filing a written application for such classification with the assessor of such municipality not earlier than thirty days before nor later than thirty days after the date of such assessment list. Such assessor shall determine whether such land is farm land and, if he determines that it is farm land, he shall classify and include it as such on such assessment list. In determining whether such land is farm land, such assessor shall take into account, among other things, the acreage of such land, the portion thereof in actual use for farming or agricultural operations, the productivity of such land, the gross income derived therefrom, the nature and value of the

143

(O)

equipment used in connection therewith, and the extent to which the tracts comprising such land are contiguous. (b) An application for classification of land as farm land shall be made upon a form prescribed by the tax commissioner and shall set forth a description of the land, a general description of the use to which it is being put, and such other information as the assessor may require to aid him in determining whether such land qualifies for such classification. (c) Failure to file an application for classification of land as farm land within the time limit prescribed in subsection (a) and in the manner and form prescribed in subsection (b) shall be considered a waiver of the right to such classification on such assessment list. (d) Any person aggrieved by the denial of any application for the classification of land as farm land shall have the same rights and remedies for appeal and relief as are provided in the general statutes for taxpayers claiming to be aggrieved by the doings of assessors or boards of tax review.

SEC. 4. (a) An owner of land may file a written application with the state forester for its designation by the state forester as forest land. When such application has been made, the state forester shall examine the land and, if he determines that it is forest land, he shall issue a triplicate certificate designating it as such, and file one copy of such certificate in his office, furnish one to the owner of the land and file one in the office of the assessor of the municipality in which the land is located. (b) When requested to do so by such assessor or whenever he deems it necessary, the state forester shall re-examine land designated by him as forest land and, if he finds that it is no longer forest land, he shall issue a triplicate certificate cancelling his designation of such land as forest land, and file one copy of such certificate in his office, furnish one to the owner of the land and file one in the office of such assessor. (c) An owner of land designated as forest land by the state forester may apply for its classification as forest land on any assessment list of a municipality by filing a written application for such classification with the assessor of such municipality not earlier than thirty days before nor later than thirty days after the date of such assessment list and, if the state forester has not cancelled his designation of such land as forest land as of a date at or prior to the date of such assessment list, such assessor shall classify such land as forest land and include it as such on such assessment list. (d) An application to the state forester for designation of land as forest land shall be made upon a form prescribed by the state forester and approved by the state tax commissioner and shall set forth a description of the land and such other information as the state forester may require to aid him in determining whether such land qualifies for such designation. An application to an assessor for classification of land as forest land shall be made upon a form prescribed by such assessor and approved by the state tax commissioner and shall set forth a description of the land, the date of the issuance by the state forester of his certificate designating it as forest land. (e) Failure to file an application for classification of land as forest land within the time limit prescribed in subsection (c) and in the manner and form prescribed in subsection (d) shall be considered a waiver of the right to such classification on such assessment list. (f) The municipality within which land designated as forest land by the state forester is situated or the owner of land which the state forester has refused to designate as such may appeal from the decision of the state forester to the court 144 of common pleas for the county within which such municipality is situated.

Such appeal shall be taken within thirty days after the issuance of the certificate designating such land as forest land or the refusal to issue such certificate, as the case may be, and shall be brought by petition in writing with proper citation signed by competent authority to the adverse party at least twelve days before the return day. The court of common pleas shall have the same powers with respect to such appeals as are provided in the general statutes with respect to appeals from boards of tax review. (g) An owner of land aggrieved by the denial of any application to the assessor of a municipality for classification of land as forest land shall have the same rights and remedies for appeal and relief as are provided in the general statutes for taxpayers claiming to be aggrieved by the doings of assessors or boards of tax review.

SEC. 5. (a) The planning commission of any municipality in preparing a plan of development for such municipality may designate upon such plan areas which it recommends for preservation as areas of open space land. Land included in any area so designated upon such plan as finally adopted may be classified as open space land for purposes of property taxation if there has been no change in the use of such area which has adversely affected its essential character as an area of open space land between the date of the adoption of such plan and the date of such classification. (b) An owner of land included in any area designated as open space land upon any plan as finally adopted may apply for its classification as open space land on any assessment list of a municipality by filing a written application for such classification with the assessor of such municipality not earlier than thirty days before nor later than thirty days after the date of such assessment list. Such assessor shall determine whether there has been any change in the area designated as an area of open space land upon the plan of development which adversely affects its essential character as an area of open space land and, if he determines that there has been no such change, he shall classify such land as open space land and include it as such on such assessment list. An application for classification of land as open space land shall be made upon a form prescribed by the tax commissioner and shall set forth a description of the land, a general description of the use to which it is being put, and such other information as the assessor may require to aid him in determining whether such land qualifies for such classification. (c) Failure to file an application for classification of land as open space land within the time limit prescribed in subsection (a) and in the manner and form prescribed in subsection (b) shall be considered a waiver of the right to such classification on such assessment list. (d) Any person aggrieved by the denial by an assessor of any application for the classification of land as open space land shall have the same rights and remedies for appeal and relief as are provided in the general statutes for taxpayers claiming to be aggrieved by the doings of assessors or boards of tax review.

SEC. 6. Any municipality may, by vote of its legislative body, by purchase, condemnation, gift, devise, lease or otherwise, acquire any land in any area designated as an area of open space land on any plan of development of a municipality adopted by its planning commission or any easements, interest, or rights therein and enter into covenants and agreements with owners of such open space land or interests therein to maintain, improve, protect, limit the future use of or otherwise conserve such open space land.

SEC. 7. Subsection (b) of section 7-131a of the 1961 supplement to the general statutes is repealed and the following is substituted in lieu thereof: 145

(O) A conservation commission shall conduct researches into the utilization and possible utilization of land areas of the municipality and may coordinate the activities of unofficial bodies organized for similar purposes, and may advertise, prepare and distribute books, maps, charts, plans and pamphlets as necessary for its purposes. It shall keep an index of all open areas, publicly or privately owned, including open marshlands, swamps and other wetlands, for the purpose of obtaining information on the proper use of such areas, and may from time to time recommend to the *planning commission or, if none, to the* chief executive officer *or* the legislative body [or the planning commission] plans and programs for the development and use of such areas, which may include the acquisition of conservation easements. It may acquire land in the name of the municipality for any of its purposes as set out in this section. It shall keep records of its meetings and activities and shall make an annual report to the municipality in the manner required of other agencies of the respective municipalities. The commission may receive gifts in the name of the municipality for any of its purposes and shall administer the same for such purposes subject to the terms of the gift.

SEC. 8. Subsection (a) of section 12-53 of the general statutes is repealed and the following is substituted in lieu thereof: The assessors of each town shall add to the list given in by any person and made according to law any taxable property which they have reason to believe is owned by him and has been omitted from such list, and property so added shall be assessed at the percentage of the actual valuation thereof, as determined by the assessors in accordance with the provisions of *section 9 of this act and* section 12-64 and 12-71, from the best information the assessors can obtain, and ten per cent of such assessment shall be added thereto.

SEC. 9. Section 12-63 of the general statutes is repealed and the following is substituted in lieu thereof: The present true and actual value of [any estate] *land classified as farm land pursuant to section 3 hereof, as forest land pursuant to section 4 hereof, or as open space land pursuant to section 5 hereof shall be based upon its current use without regard to neighborhood land use of a more intensive nature, provided in no event shall the present true and actual value of open space land be less than it would be if such open space land comprised a part of a tract or tracts of land classified as farm land pursuant to section 3 hereof. The present true and actual value of all other property* shall be deemed by all assessors and boards of tax review to be the fair market value thereof and not its value at a forced or auction sale.

SEC. 10. Section 12-76 of the general statutes is repealed and the following is substituted in lieu thereof: Land owned or taken by any municipal corporation for the purpose of creating or furnishing a supply of water for its use shall be exempt from taxation when the inhabitants of the town in which such land is situated have the right to use, and use, such water supply upon the same terms as the inhabitants of such municipal corporation; otherwise such land shall be liable to taxation and shall be assessed in the town in which such land is situated to the corporation owning or controlling such water supply *at what would be its fair market value were it improved farm land* [at the average assessed valuation per acre of the improved farming land in such town].

SEC. 11. Section 12-78 of the general statutes is repealed and the following is substituted in lieu thereof: When such power is appropriated and used

146

in any other town than that in which the dam, canal, reservoir or pond creating it is located, the valuation of the land occupied by such dam, canal, reservoir or pond, and the increased flowage occasioned thereby, shall be made and set in the list in the town in which such dam, canal, reservoir or pond is located, to the owner of such power at *what would be its fair market value were it improved farm land* [the average assessed valuation of improved farming land in such town], and such power shall be assessed and set in the list in the town in which it is so used and appropriated as incidental to the machinery which is operated by it, and not separately as distinct property. The assessors shall, in estimating either the incidental value of such power to the machinery operated by it, or its net rental value, deduct from the amount which would otherwise be assessed against such power the value of the land so occupied.

SEC. 12.   Section 12-109 of the general statutes is repealed and the following is substituted in lieu thereof: All property exempted from taxation under the provisions of any special act shall be valued annually by the assessors of the town in which such property is located in the same manner as *provided for the valuation of property other than land classified as farm land, forest land or open space land* [other property] and such valuation shall be added by the assessors to the abstract book.

SEC. 13.   Sections 7-131b, 12-104, 12-105, 12-106 and 12-107 are repealed.

SEC. 14.   This act shall take effect from its passage.

(P)

THE COMMONWEALTH OF MASSACHUSETTS
CONSERVATION COMMISSION ACT

Chapter 40, Section 8C:—A city or town which accepts this section may establish a conservation commission, hereinafter called the commission, for the promotion and development of the natural resources and for the protection of the watershed resources of said city or town. Such commission shall conduct researches into its local land areas and shall seek to coordinate the activities of unofficial bodies organized for similar purposes, and may advertise, prepare, print and distribute books, maps, charts, plans and pamphlets which in its judgment it deems necessary for its work. It shall keep an index of all open areas within the city or town, as the case may be, with the plan of obtaining information pertinent to proper utilization of such open areas, including lands owned by the commonwealth or lands owned by a city or town. It shall keep an index of all open marsh lands, swamps and all other wet lands in a like manner, and may recommend to the city council or selectmen and, subject to the approval of the city council or selectmen, to the department of natural resources and to the state reclamation board, a program for the better promotion, development or utilization of all such areas. It shall keep accurate records of its meetings and actions and shall file an annual report which shall be printed in the case of towns in the annual town report. The commission may appoint such clerks and other employees as it may from time to time require. The commission shall consist of not less than three nor more than seven members. In cities the members shall be appointed by the mayor, subject to the provisions of the city charter, except that in cities having or operating under a Plan D or Plan E form of city charter, said appointments shall be by the city manager, subject to the provisions of the charter; and in towns they shall be appointed by the selectmen, excepting towns having a manager form of government, in which town appointments shall be made by the town manager, subject to the approval of the selectmen. When a commission is first established, terms of the members shall be for one, two or three years, and so arranged that the terms of approximately one-third of the members will expire each year, and their successors shall be appointed for terms of three years each. Any member of a commission so appointed may, after a public hearing, if requested, be removed for cause by the appointing authority. A vacancy occurring otherwise than by expiration of a term shall in a city be filled for the unexpired term in the same manner as an original appointment and in a town in the manner provided in section eleven of chapter forty-one. Said commission may receive gifts of property, both real and personal, in the name of the city or town, subject to the approval of the city council in a city or the selectmen in a town, such gifts to be managed and controlled by the commission for the purposes of this section. Said commission may acquire by gift, purchase, grant, bequest, devise, lease or otherwise the fee in such land or water rights, or any lesser interest, development right, easement, covenant, or other contractual right including conveyances on conditions or with limitations or reversions, as may be necessary to acquire, maintain, improve, protect, limit the future use of or otherwise conserve and properly utilize open spaces and other land and water areas within their city or town and shall manage and control the same. For the purposes of this section a city or town may, upon the written request of the commission, take by eminent domain under chapter

148

seventy-nine, the fee or any lesser interest in any land or waters located in such city or town, provided such taking has first been approved by a two-thirds vote of the city council or a two-thirds vote of an annual or special town meeting, which land and waters shall thereupon be under the jurisdiction and control of the commission. The commission may adopt rules and regulations governing the use of land and waters under its control, and prescribe penalties, not exceeding a fine of one hundred dollars, for any violation thereof. No action taken under this section shall affect the powers and duties of the state reclamation board or any mosquito control or other project operating under or authorized by chapter two hundred and fifty-two, or restrict any established public access. Lands used for farming or agriculture, as defined in section one A of chapter one hundred and twenty-eight, shall not be taken by eminent domain under the authority of this section.

11/21/66

Chapter 885

AN ACT authorizing cities and towns to expend monies from the Conservation Fund to pay damages for the taking of property by eminent domain for conservation purposes.

SECTION 8C of Chapter 40 of the General Laws is hereby amended by inserting after the fourteenth sentence, inserted by Section 2 of Chapter 768 of the Acts of 1965, the following sentence:—Upon a like vote, a city or town may expend monies in the fund, if any, established under the provisions of clause (51) of Section five for the purpose of paying, in whole or in part, any damages for which such city or town may be liable by reason of any such taking.

APPROVED: January 5, 1968

CONNECTICUT CONSERVATION COMMISSION
ENABLING LEGISLATION

(excerpts from Chapter 97 of the Connecticut General Statutes, 1963 revision)

SEC. 7-131a. Conservation commissions. (a) Any town, city or borough, by vote of its legislative body, may establish a conservation commission for the development and conservation of natural resources, including water resources, within its territorial limits. The commission shall consist of not fewer than three nor more than seven members, to be appointed by the chief executive officer of the municipality, to serve for terms to be designated by the legislative body establishing the commission. The chief executive officer may remove any member for cause and may fill any vacancy. (b) A conservation commission shall conduct research into the utilization and possible utilization of land areas of the municipality and may coordinate the activities of unofficial bodies organized for similar purposes, and may advertise, prepare and distribute books, maps, charts, plans and pamphlets as necessary for its purposes. It shall keep an index of all open areas, publicly or privately owned, including open marshlands, swamps and other wetlands, for the purpose of obtaining information on the proper use of such areas, and may from time to time recommend to the *planning commission or, if none, to the* chief executive officer *or* the legislative body * * * plans and programs for the development and use of such areas, which may include the acquisition of conservation easements. It may acquire land in the name of the municipality for any of its purposes as set out in this section. It shall keep records of its meetings and activities and shall make an annual report to the municipality in the manner required of other agencies of the respective municipalities. The commission may receive gifts in the name of the municipality for any of its purposes and shall administer the same for such purposes subject to the terms of the gift. (1961, P.A. 310; 1963, P.A. 490, S. 7.) Effective June 24, 1963.

NEW YORK CONSERVATION ADVISORY COUNCIL ENABLING LEGISLATION

(R)

The People of the State of New York, represented in Senate and Assembly, do enact as follows:

SECTION 1. The town law is hereby amended by inserting therein a new section, to be section sixty-four-b, to read as follows:

§64b. Town conservation advisory council. The town board of each town is hereby authorized and empowered to appoint a conservation advisory council, hereinafter called the council to advise in the promotion and development of its natural resources. Such council shall conduct researches into the land area of the town and shall seek to coordinate the activities of unofficial bodies organized for similar purposes and may advertise, prepare, print and distribute books, maps, charts, plans and pamphlets which in its judgment it deems necessary for its work. It shall keep an index of all open areas within the town with the plan of obtaining information pertinent to proper utilization of such open areas including lands owned by the state or lands owned by a village within the town or lands owned by the town. It shall keep an index of all open marshlands, swamps and all other wet lands in a like manner, and may recommend to the town board and, subject to the approval of the town board, to the New York state department of conservation, a program for the better promotion, development or utilization of all such areas. It shall keep accurate records of its meetings and actions and shall file an annual report which shall be printed in the annual town report.

The council shall consist of not less than five nor more than nine members who shall be appointed by the town board for a term not exceeding two years. The presiding officer or chairman of the council shall be designated by the town board from among the members so appointed to the council. The town board shall have authority to remove any member of said council so appointed for cause, after a public hearing, if requested. A vacancy shall be filled for the unexpired term in the same manner as an original appointment. The town board may provide for compensation to be paid to the member of the council and is also empowered and authorized to make such appropriations as it may see fit for such expenses incurred by the council. The council may appoint such clerks and other employees as it may from time to time require with the approval of the town board. The services and expenses of the council shall not exceed the appropriation that may be made therefor by the town board. Such salaries, charges and expenses so permitted by an appropriation of the town board shall be a charge upon the taxable property of that part of the town outside of incorporated villages and shall be assessed, levied and collected therefrom in the same manner as other town charges.

§2. This act shall take effect immediately.